English Language Learners

▪The Essential Guide▪

David Freeman
& Yvonne Freeman

■SCHOLASTIC

New York • Toronto • London • Auckland • Sydney
Mexico City • New Delhi • Hong Kong • Buenos Aires

Acknowledgments

Over the years, as we have researched the best ways to work effectively with English language learners, we have relied on both the theories we have read and the teachers who have been our students and whose classrooms we have visited. We have used many examples from their teaching as we have written this book. We wish to acknowledge their contributions to our growing understanding of how theory translates into practice. It is classroom teachers who continue to remind us of both the joys and challenges of working with English language learners on a daily basis.

We also wish to thank Lois Bridges, our editor. Lois is always supportive. She supported our interest in undertaking this project and followed the progress of the writing closely at every step. In addition, we wish to thank Maria L. Chang, who worked to ensure that the many details involved in the production of the book were completed.

Dedication

We dedicate this book to family members: our daughter, Mary; our son-in-law, Francisco; and our daughter, Ann; and her new husband, Chris. Many classroom examples come from Mary and Francisco's classrooms. Ann now is also a teacher educator, and she has provided us with new resources and a renewed sense of mission. Chris' strong Greek roots have reminded us how important it is for our English language learners to cherish their customs and traditions as they also embrace those of this country.

Editor: Lois Bridges
Cover design by Norma Ortiz
Interior design by Jeffrey Dorman
Cover: bottom: Will Hart/PhotoEdit Inc.; all others: Photodisc via SODA; p. 5: © FogStock LLC/IndexOpen; p. 12: © Blend/Getty Images; p. 33: Francisco Soto; p. 61: © FogStock LLC/IndexOpen; p. 81: © Jeff Greenberg/PhotoEdit Inc.; p. 119: David Freeman; p. 147: © Gabe Palmer/Corbis

ISBN-13: 978-0-439-92646-1
ISBN-10: 0-439-92646-7
Copyright © 2007 by David Freeman and Yvonne Freeman
All rights reserved. Printed in the USA.

3 4 5 6 7 8 9 10   40   15 14 13 12 11 10 09 08

Table of Contents

Introduction

Challenges Schools Face

School administrators, curriculum specialists, and classroom teachers all have the same goal: to enable every student to succeed academically. This has always been the mission of schools, but now government mandates require districts to submit test results for each subgroup of students, proving that they meet or exceed the standards set by state and federal guidelines. One of these subgroups consists of students with *limited English proficiency* (LEP). In the past, these *English language learners* (ELLs) were often excluded from state or national tests, but now they are given only a short time to learn English, usually just one or two years, before they are tested in English in reading, mathematics, science, and social studies.

Some states, such as California, Texas, New York, Florida, and Illinois, have had large numbers of ELLs in the public school system for many years. Other states have had only small and scattered pockets of *second language students*, often concentrated in one or two schools. Even in states with large numbers of ELLs, districts and schools vary widely in the number of LEP students they serve.

Despite these differences between and within states, one fact stands out: the number of ELLs is increasing dramatically. According to statistics compiled by the National Clearinghouse for English Language Acquisition (NCELA) (www.ncela.gwu.edu, 2006) in the 1994–95 school year, the K–12 enrollment in U.S. schools was 47.75 million students. Of these, a little more than 3 million, or about 7 percent, were ELLs. Ten years later, in the 2003–04 school year, the total number of students in U.S. schools was 48.98 million, an increase of just 2.59 percent. During that same period, the ELL population had soared to more than 5 million, a 61 percent gain. In 2004, one in every ten students was an English language learner. Nearly every state recorded gains in their ELL population. Eleven states reported a greater than 200 percent increase in ELLs during the ten-year period.

The U.S. Census Bureau reports that about one in five students in public schools lives in a home where English is not the primary language. The Bureau predicts that by 2030, nearly 40 percent of the school-age population will speak a language other than English at home. One reason for this increase is the number of refugees that have come to the United States. The government allocated resources for 70,000 refugees for the 2005–06 fiscal year. About 44 percent of the refugees are under the age of 18, and many have had limited or interrupted schooling.

About one in five students in public schools lives in a home where English is not the primary language.

G. García (2000) points out that ELLs, both recent immigrants and those born in the United States, are less likely than mainstream students to have had the kind of early pre-reading supports that teachers expect, such as being read to aloud, using educational games and toys, inventing stories, and reciting rhymes. In addition, they often live in households and neighborhoods with high and sustained poverty, attend schools with other poor children, and are members of families that are likely to move from one school or district to another at least once during the school year. Parents of ELLs want to help their children succeed in school, but many of them work long hours to support their families and lack the necessary educational background and English skills they need to assist their children. Not surprisingly, national statistics show that ELLs are three times as likely as native English speakers to be low academic achievers. They are also twice as likely to be held back to repeat

a grade. These statistics point to the challenges schools face in meeting their goal of enabling every student to succeed academically.

The rapid growth in the ELL population has left many districts searching for teachers with the experience and training to work effectively with second language students. In some states, many teachers have received at least some training in working with ELLs while in other states, fewer teachers have had adequate preparation for working with second language students. The No Child Left Behind Act (NCLB) requires that students be taught by well-qualified teachers, but in areas with rapid population growth and a shortage of teachers, certification programs often include only a limited amount of instruction on the theory and research that supports effective instruction for ELLs.

We have written this book to help administrators, curriculum specialists, and classroom teachers meet the challenge of working effectively with their increasing numbers of LEP students. Learning English and, at the same time, developing the knowledge and skills needed in the different content areas takes time. There is no magic bullet. Nevertheless, there are more and less effective approaches and practices for working with second language students. In the chapters that follow, we outline the theory and explain and illustrate with classroom examples the instructional approaches that work best for ELLs. We hope the guidelines we offer here will enable districts to meet the goal of helping all their students, including their English language learners, to succeed academically.

Types of Programs for ELLs

Depending on their student population, districts have developed different kinds of programs to meet the needs of ELLs. In this section, we provide a brief overview of the most common kinds of programs that are offered.

Bilingual Education

In areas with large numbers of ELLs from one language background, a common program design is some model of bilingual education. Although bilingual programs vary considerably, they all provide some instruction in the students' native language as well as instruction in English. *Transitional programs* offer two or three years of first-language support. During the time they are learning English, students in transitional programs receive instruction in the different content areas in their native language. This allows them to keep up in language arts, mathematics, social studies, and science as they learn English. Once students can speak and understand English, first-language instruction is dropped and students are transitioned into an all-English program.

Maintenance bilingual programs extend for a longer period of time, usually five or six years. Students continue to receive some instruction in their first language, even after they speak and understand English. The goal of a maintenance program is to teach students English and also develop their first language to a level that allows them to read and write as well as speak and understand two languages well.

More recently, many *two-way immersion* or *dual language programs* have been implemented (Y. Freeman et al., 2005). In these programs, all students learn a second language. Both native English speakers and English language learners receive instruction in two languages at least through the elementary years and sometimes into middle and high school. Dual language programs have shown great promise for both high academic achievement and positive cross-cultural understanding. Several different dual language models have been developed. Even though the programs have often shown success, they must be well implemented and well staffed.

In many parts of the world, bilingual or multilingual education is the norm. Bilingual education has solid research support (Greene, 1998; Rolstad et al., 2005; Willig, 1985). However, in the United States there has been strong opposition to bilingual education during different historical periods, including the present time (Crawford, 2004). As a result, in many districts, bilingual programs are closely scrutinized and must show immediate positive results. In addition, many districts have ELLs from different language backgrounds, and a bilingual program would not meet the needs of all their second language students. Further, in parts of the country schools find it difficult to recruit bilingual teachers. Nearly 73 percent of urban school districts have an immediate need for bilingual teachers. For these reasons, most ELLs are served by some type of *English as a Second Language* (ESL) program.

English as a Second Language (ESL) Education

Districts often establish a *newcomer center* to serve students who enter school with little or no English. In newcomer centers, ESL teachers provide initial instruction in English as well as an orientation to U.S. schools. Students may stay in these centers for several weeks or several months. They are then placed in schools where they continue to receive some ESL support, either from a specialist or from the regular classroom teacher. In areas with fewer ELLs, newcomers are enrolled directly into mainstream classes. The classroom teacher may provide them with all their instruction, or they may be pulled out for instruction by an ESL teacher. At the secondary level, ELLs may receive one or two periods of ESL along with their regular classes. In addition, schools may hire paraprofessionals to support the ESL instruction. Often, these are individuals who speak the native languages of the children.

Traditional ESL focuses on helping students develop the basic vocabulary and grammar needed to communicate in English. Students are taught the vocabulary of clothing or food, for example. ESL teachers use various techniques to help students gain enough English to function in an English-speaking environment. A common strategy is *Total Physical Response* (TPR). During a TPR lesson, the teacher gives commands like "Touch your nose," and the student demonstrates understanding by performing the action (Asher, 1977).

In most schools, traditional approaches to ESL have been replaced by *content-based ESL instruction*. Rather than focusing on basic vocabulary and grammar, teachers modify instruction in mathematics, science, or social studies and teach English through the content area. By doing this, they provide both English and academic content instruction at the same time. However, it does take a skilled teacher to modify lessons so that ESL students with different levels of English proficiency can understand the instruction. This is an especially challenging task for the regular classroom teacher with one or a few ELLs in a class of many native speakers.

Some states, such as California and Arizona, passed laws requiring that all instruction of ELLs be in English using an approach referred to as *Structured English Immersion* (SEI). This method is similar to content-based ESL, but teachers are seldom given much training in how to implement the method. Since students don't receive specialized ESL instruction in SEI classes, success depends entirely on how well teachers can accommodate the needs of a variety of students with varying levels of English and academic proficiency. SEI is a new approach, and to date no research supports this method of instructing ELLs.

Many different approaches and instructional models have been implemented to teach ELLs. We have given only a brief overview of the most common methods. For a more thorough discussion of bilingual and ESL methods, see our book *ESL/EFL Teaching: Principles for Success* (Y. Freeman & D. Freeman, 1998). We have written the present book, *English Language Learners: The Essential Guide,* primarily for regular classroom teachers with one or more ELLs in their class. Our goal is to provide the help these teachers need to work effectively with their second language students. In the following chapters, we explain the theories that underlie good instruction for second language students and then show how those theories can be put into action in lower- and upper-grade classrooms. At the end of each chapter, we provide applications to help readers connect the contents to their own contexts.

Organization of This Book

Each chapter of this book focuses on one key for working successfully with ELLs. The first key is "Know your students." We begin Chapter 1 by describing the ELL population in four districts. Two are urban districts, and two are rural. Each district has a different ELL population. The first has many recent refugees; the second has many ELLs from a variety of language backgrounds. The third has only a few ELLs, and the last district has a high concentration of Latino students. Our hope is that teachers will find that one district is similar to theirs. Next we describe differences among ELLs. Some are recent arrivals with adequate schooling background, others are newcomers with limited formal schooling, and a third group has lived in the United States for many years but still struggles with English. Knowing a student's background is the first step in effective instruction. We conclude the first chapter by considering the contextual factors within and beyond the school that contribute to students' academic performance.

The second key is "Teach language through content." In Chapter 2, we explain how teachers can teach both language and content at the same time. We provide reasons for this approach, and we outline an important theory of second language acquisition that supports content-based language teaching. In this and the following chapters, we describe two lessons or units, one from a lower-grade classroom and one from an upper grade, to illustrate the principle.

"Organize curriculum around themes," the third key, is the topic of Chapter 3. We discuss reasons why organizing around themes, even at upper grades, supports ELLs. Chapter 4 shows how to "Draw on students' primary languages and cultures," even when the teacher doesn't speak the language. In this chapter, we also review an important theory that is the basis for drawing on students' first languages. As in other chapters, we suggest specific strategies teachers can use to implement the key.

The fifth chapter focuses on literacy. The key is to "Emphasize meaningful reading and writing." Often, ELLs become good decoders of English but fail to construct meaning from English texts. As they advance through the grades, they experience great difficulty, especially in content area reading. We suggest ways teachers can organize literacy instruction and develop text sets to help ELLs make sense of reading in English.

In the final chapter, we turn to the important topic of academic language. ELLs, like other students, need to "Develop academic language" in order to succeed in school. We suggest ways teachers can scaffold instruction to support ELLs so they can meet the challenge of reading, writing, and discussing academic content. We also explain how teachers can develop language and content objectives and plan lessons that both challenge and support their ELLs.

Many teachers have ELLs in their classes. The keys we present in this book are designed to help these teachers provide the best possible instruction for all their students, and especially for their ELLs. When teachers gather information about their second language students, teach language through content, organize curriculum around themes, draw on students' languages and cultures, emphasize meaningful reading, and use strategies to help students develop academic language, their ELLs receive the help they need to succeed academically. The task for ELLs and for teachers is not an easy one, but it is our hope that the keys presented in this book will guide teachers toward best practices for their second language students.

CHAPTER 1

Know Your Students

Across the country, many teachers find that they have one or more English Language Learners (ELLs) in their classrooms. These students face a double challenge: They must learn English, and they must learn *in* English. They need to develop the same grade-level content knowledge as their native English-speaking peers. Teachers often worry that they are not doing what is best for their second language learners. Programs and specific strategies for working with ELLs are useful, but they are not always enough. Teachers need to understand their students, second language acquisition theory, and best practices in order to be effective. When teachers ask us what is most important for working with ELLs, we always tell them, "Know your students." English language learners vary a great deal, and in order to teach them well, it is critically important to know who they are, where they have come from, and what strengths they bring with them to the classroom.

We begin this chapter by describing four school districts with differing ELL populations. Next, we describe three different kinds of English language learners, giving the characteristics of each and introducing some of the instructional needs they have. As teachers get to know their students, they must also consider the social context. We describe a model that illustrates the many factors that influence second language students' learning. As you read about these districts and students, think about how they are the same as and how they are different from the district where you work and the ELLs in your school.

Large Numbers of ELLs in a Large Urban District

Fresno Unified School District, located in the middle of the Central Valley of California, is the fourth largest district in the state. With almost 80,000 students in 2004–05—eight high schools, 19 middle schools, and 61 elementary schools—the district faces almost all the challenges any large, urban district in the country might encounter. More than one-third of the students, or about 24,500, are identified as English language learners. The home language survey identified 76 different home languages (webmaster@fresno.k12.ca.us). After the Vietnam War, the district received large numbers of Southeast Asian refugees. Most were Hmong, rural-nomadic people granted asylum in this country because they supported the CIA during the war. In 1994–95 the district had more than 17,000 Asian students, 22 percent of the total school population, and the majority were from refugee families. Now, ten years later, the district receives newcomers mainly from Mexico and Thailand, but few are refugees. Hispanics make up 55.2 percent of the minority population, an increase of 40.5 percent from ten years ago. The overall Asian population of the district has dropped to just under 11 percent. The most recent refugee population has been Hmong, who have come after the closing of the last refugee camps in Thailand. However, at present, the majority of the district's ELL students were born in the United States. Most of these students come to school speaking Spanish, Hmong, Khmer (the language of Cambodia), or Lao, but within a year or two, English becomes their dominant language. While these students speak English without an accent, many often struggle academically.

The district requires that all teachers, including mainstream teachers, have certification to work with English learners. This may be through a state examination or university coursework. However, more than 600 elementary and secondary teachers still do not have appropriate authorization to work with ELLs. The district-level ELL resource specialists are very knowledgeable and provide workshops throughout the year that teachers attend to receive professional development credit. Still, teachers in the district are concerned that they have limited resources to draw upon to help them work with their second language learners.

Providing support for teachers working with English language learners in this large district is challenging, particularly after the passage of several pieces of legislation that severely limit choices of appropriate curriculum and prohibit using the students' first languages to give them access to content. California has no clear guidelines concerning materials, approaches, and time frames for teaching ELLs, and instruction for ELLs is often "embedded" in the mainstream reading program. The district uses Structured English Immersion (SEI) to help ELLs develop English. In this SEI program, ELLs receive a half hour of explicit *English language development* (ELD) instruction, but the district has not adopted a specific ELD program. Some elementary schools have bought a program to use during ELD time, and then support ELLs with different strategies during the rest of the day. However, in such a large district, it is difficult to monitor the implementation and effectiveness of the various approaches.

Factors beyond the school also affect the education of ELLs in Fresno. The city of Fresno has the highest concentration of families living in poverty of any city in the country (http://www.brookings.edu/metro/pubs/20051012_concentratedpoverty.htm). New Orleans ranks second. Because of economic and social problems in the inner city, many students join gangs. In addition, teachers struggle to make curriculum accessible because the state-mandated programs were developed to meet the needs of native English speakers. High-stakes testing discourages both students and teachers, and many students drop out.

Large Numbers of Refugees in an Urban District

Minnesota is a state known for encouraging refugee settlement. Of the immigrants who come to Minnesota, 24 percent are refugees compared to 8 percent nationally. Minneapolis and St. Paul, two adjoining cities known as the Twin Cities, together have the largest Somali and Hmong populations and the second largest Southeast Asian population in the country. The two cities also have the largest Tibetan population outside of Tibet.

St. Paul Public Schools (SPPS), Minnesota's second largest school district, with more than 41,000 students, is known as a district that welcomes newcomers from all over the world. The student population is 27 percent Caucasian American, 30 percent Asian American, 29 percent African American, and 13 percent Hispanic American. In 2005–06, the ELL population was the largest in the state, with almost 17,000 identified second language learners representing 42 percent of the entire student body (SPPS, 2006). Students in the district speak 103 different languages and dialects other than English including Hmong, Spanish, Somali, Vietnamese, Burmese, Amharic, and Oromo.

The district offers many different content-based ESL programs for these newcomers from kindergarten age through age 21. These programs have the double goal of helping students develop English language proficiency and, at the same time, learn subject-area content. However, the challenges are great. Many refugees come with interrupted or very limited schooling, and once here, they face cultural, social, and economic adjustments. The district makes many efforts to incorporate students' culture into the curriculum. An example of this that has attracted attention nationally is the embedding of the Somali culture in the K–3 social studies curriculum. The St. Paul Public Schools ELL Department has developed a handbook about Somalia and its people, and teachers receive materials including lesson plans to embed elements of Somali culture in the social studies curriculum. The materials include books in Somali and English, DVDs, CDs, and cultural items. Programs have also been developed to embed elements of Hmong and Latino culture in the elementary social studies curriculum (http://www.spps.org).

Despite these efforts, there is more work to be done. Teachers need specialized training that includes both second language acquisition theory and best practices to meet the needs of their ever-changing student population. Relevant and appropriate materials for the diverse students are critical and sometimes difficult to find. Perhaps the greatest challenge is to offer students academically challenging curriculum while, at the same time, helping them catch up with both English and content learning.

Small Numbers of ELLs in a Small City

Harrisburg, Pennsylvania, is located about halfway between Pittsburgh and Philadelphia. The population is just under 50,000, and the school district has approximately 7,700 students. More than 1,000 of the students come to school speaking a language other than English, but only a little more than half of these students receive ESL services (Harrisburg School District, 2006). The ELL population in Pennsylvania is representative of many states in the country where the number of ELL students has increased dramatically. Between 1994–95 and 2004–05, 11 states, including Pennsylvania, recorded increases in their ELL population of 100 to 200 percent while another 11 states had more than a 200 percent growth in their ELL population. In Pennsylvania, the total K–12 enrollment has decreased, and even though the number of ELLs has increased, they still make up only about 2 percent of the total school population. States like Pennsylvania are said to have a *"small and scattered" ELL population*. The ELLs are often concentrated in a single district, such as Harrisburg.

Harrisburg has students from 22 different language groups with the majority speaking Spanish, Vietnamese, Arabic, Indonesian, and Khmer. The district has made some special efforts to help teachers and administrators through an easily accessible Web site that includes a PowerPoint presentation containing some basic second language acquisition theory and suggestions for appropriate classroom practices (http://www.hbgsd.k12.pa.us/20437548125949/). As the population of non-English speakers continues to grow, more educators in the district will find the need to learn what they can do to help ELLs succeed.

Pennsylvania and other states with this recent ELL population growth spurt are just beginning to understand the need to devote attention to supporting these students. While local workshops and state and national conferences are sources for professional development, only a few teachers and administrators commit to learning about second language acquisition and teaching second language learners, especially when they do not have large numbers of ELLs in their schools. Often, instruction for students in areas with small and scattered populations is relegated to an aide in a pull-out situation. This is less than ideal since the students do not receive support from a highly qualified teacher that would enable them to succeed academically.

Large Numbers of ELLs in a Rural District

Donna Independent School District is located in the Rio Grande Valley along the Mexican border of South Texas. The school population of this rural, agriculturally based community is slightly over 13,000, and 53 percent of the students have been identified as limited English proficient. Ninety-nine percent of the students are Hispanic, and 93 percent are identified as economically disadvantaged. Most of the Hispanic students are of Mexican origin, and many of them cross the border frequently. Spanish and English are heard in the schools and in the community. Most teachers are Hispanic, have been raised in the Rio Grande Valley, and come from the city of Donna or surrounding communities. Many are at least somewhat bilingual, although many speak what is referred to as Tex-Mex, a dialect of Spanish unique to the area.

Most schools in the district have used transitional bilingual education programs at the elementary level. Students entering school not speaking English are given some support in content areas in Spanish but encouraged to transition into English within two to three years. This early transition into English has produced many students who speak English but struggle with reading and writing in upper elementary and secondary classrooms. Many students become discouraged and drop out of school. In Donna, as in many other school districts in South Texas, only about half the students who enter seventh grade graduate six years later, although officially reported dropout rates are generally lower.

These numbers are disturbing because the district also receives many newcomers of varying ages each year. Some come with adequate schooling, but many do not. Test scores in the district have generally been low. One elementary school has been the exception. That school implemented a whole-school dual language program in which students received approximately half of their instruction in English and half in Spanish. This program was carefully implemented with knowledgeable teachers. The success of this program attracted local, state, and national attention.

The district has developed a plan to implement dual language in all 13 elementary schools from pre-kindergarten through grade 5 as well as in the three middle schools. At the high school, teachers are to receive specialized training in sheltered English techniques. Recently, surrounding districts have shown interest in following a similar dual language plan themselves, and representatives from even the large metropolis of Dallas have visited the district and adopted a similar plan for many of their schools. This interest has encouraged and excited those in Donna and strengthened community, school board, teacher, and administrative commitment to their plan to implement dual language throughout the district. As one bilingual administrative team member stated, "The direction of dual language is set." However, implementation has been difficult. There has been opposition from those who do not understand dual language or the importance of developing a student's first language to accelerate the acquisition of English.

What is happening in these four districts is representative of what is happening in districts across the country. Some schools have had ELLs for many years, and others have recently begun to enroll greater numbers of second language learners. In some districts, the ELL population is very diverse, with students from different countries who speak different languages. In other districts, the majority of the students are native Spanish speakers. However, the differences among ELLs go beyond their cultural and linguistic backgrounds. When considering how best to serve ELLs, it is critical that educators understand their previous experiences. What students bring to the classroom has a strong influence on their academic achievement.

Types of English Language Learners

"Kim and Francisco are newcomers and are learning to read and write English very well, better than students who have been here since kindergarten!"

"What do I do with these new refugee students from Somalia? I don't think they have been to school at all!"

"My new students from Pakistan seem to be doing very well. Some even speak some English already!"

These comments and questions are typical of those we hear from teachers across the country. ELLs enter classes at different ages. Some do very well, while many struggle. Teaching these diverse students is complex. G. García (2000), in a review of the research on concerns about English language learners, points out that "There is no typical LEP child" (p. 3). It is important that teachers consider some basic differences among English language learners as they plan instruction for them, including differences in their academic background and their academic language proficiency. Below we describe three types of learners, providing specific examples for each.

Students With Adequate Formal Schooling – Stephanie

Estefanía, or Stephanie as she is now called, came to the United States with her parents from Argentina when she was in the second grade. She had attended a private school in Argentina and had even studied some basic English there. Both parents are educated professionals. Her mother is bilingual in English and Spanish, has an M.A. in Spanish linguistics, and operated her own ballet school before coming to the United States. Her father, who owned a successful travel agency in Argentina, speaks German and French in addition to English and Spanish.

The family, concerned about the growing economic uncertainty in Argentina, came to the United States supported by International Rotary, an organization that promotes international understanding. As soon as they arrived, Stephanie's parents sought advice from professionals in their community, and they carefully selected schools and extracurricular activities that would help their daughter succeed socially and academically. They monitored Stephanie's academic progress and communicated often with her teachers.

Stephanie acquired conversational English quickly. Her school experiences and extracurricular activities soon made her the most proficient user of conversational English in her household. Within one year, it was Stephanie's voice on the home answering machine. Her English sounded more native-like than that of her parents, even though both of them spoke English well. Stephanie also developed academic English within a short time. By fourth grade, she was already doing very well in her classes. Now, Stephanie is a junior in high school and excelling in college preparatory coursework. Her parents' main concern is that she is too much like a typical U.S. adolescent!

Stephanie represents one of three types of English learners described by Olsen and Jaramillo (1999). She was a *new arrival with adequate formal schooling*. She came to the United States with a strong educational background and literacy in her first language. She had already developed academic language in Spanish, which served as a strong base for the development of academic English. She also started school in the United States with grade-level knowledge from the different content areas, and this knowledge transferred to her subject-area studies in English. In addition, Stephanie's parents provided both encouragement and academic support.

Students like Stephanie fit into traditionally organized English as a Second Language (ESL) programs and often are integrated into the mainstream after one or two years. Teachers often ask why all their ELLs don't succeed as quickly as these students. The answer lies in looking at the differences between Stephanie's background and the backgrounds of other types of ELLs.

Students With Limited and Interrupted Schooling – Guillermo and Osman

Guillermo represents a different type of ELL. His father came to the United States from Mexico and found seasonal work picking vegetables and fruits in Texas, California, and Oregon. After several years, he sent for his wife and four children. Now, the family spends from January to May in California and May to November in Oregon working various crops. December is spent visiting relatives in Mexico.

Based on his age, Guillermo was put into a fifth-grade class when he first arrived in California. He came with little formal schooling because the rural school near his home in Mexico rarely had a teacher. In the United States, Guillermo's family follows the crops from California to Oregon, so his schooling continues to be inconsistent. Guillermo's parents are concerned about the schooling he has missed and his progress in school. They talk to his teachers often, and although they cannot give him much academic support, they volunteer to help the teacher with various classroom activities whenever they have free time. Guillermo's current teacher in California understands the gaps in his education and is working to help him catch up in English and academics. At the same time, the schooling Guillermo missed in Mexico and his interrupted schooling in the United States have made it difficult for him to develop grade-level academic English or content area knowledge and skills.

When Osman entered middle school at age 12, it was the first formal schooling experience he had ever had. He and his mother had left Somalia with his uncle and aunt and four cousins when he was 5. His father was killed during one of the many clan conflicts within the country. Osman and his family lived in a refugee camp in Kenya where schooling was extremely limited. At times, children attended classes during the morning, sitting on the ground and repeating lessons after the teacher. However, most of the time in the camps was spent trying to obtain the basic necessities to stay alive. Osman and his cousins stood in line for food and water for many hours.

Osman is typical of the Somalis who have been displaced since the late 1980s. In 2004, officials estimated that between 1 million and 3 million Somalis were living abroad, and many had immigrated to Europe, Canada, and the United States. Osman's family settled in the Minneapolis-St. Paul area, home to the largest number of Somali refugees in the United States.

For Osman and many of the other refugee children, life in the big city was overwhelming. It was a shock to move from a refugee camp with no modern conveniences, where thousands of people slept on the ground, to a large U.S. city with tall buildings, public transportation, and modern technology. For the first time in his life, Osman held a pen and kept his own books in a locker. The challenges for Osman were daunting. He had to learn English and learn the content of his classes at the same time. Although he brought many experiences with him, those were not the experiences that helped him understand the school system and the expectations the system had for him. His family could not help him very much because they had so many adjustments to make coming to a new country, looking for jobs, and finding a new home. In addition, the customs were very different in the new place. People who came in contact with Somalis did not understand many of the Muslim practices Osman and the other refugees followed. Although Osman worked hard and learned quite a bit of English in his first year in school, he realized that he was significantly behind his native English-speaking peers.

Guillermo and Osman represent a second group of students: *recent arrivals with limited or interrupted formal schooling*. These students come to school in this country with limited academic knowledge and limited English proficiency. Students like Guillermo and Osman struggle with reading and writing in English. They arrive with only minimal native language literacy. In addition, they lack basic concepts in the different subject areas. For example, they are often at least two years below grade level in areas that are not heavily language-dependent, such as performing math computations.

Limited-formal-schooling students are faced with the complex task of developing conversational English, becoming literate in English, and gaining the academic knowledge and skills they need to compete with native English speakers. Because they do not have the academic background to draw upon in their native languages, they often struggle with coursework in English and receive low scores on standardized tests. Many also lack an understanding of how schools are organized and how students are expected to act in school.

Long-Term English Learners – Kou and José

Kou, a Hmong sixth grader who has attended schools in the inner city since kindergarten, is an example of a *long-term English learner*. He was born in the United States, has never visited his native country, speaks little of his native language, and has trouble relating to or even understanding his parents and grandparents, who speak mainly Hmong. When Kou began school he spoke only Hmong. His classmates included students who spoke Hmong, Spanish, Khmer, and Russian. Kou's teachers worked hard to help Kou and his classmates with the occasional help of a bilingual Hmong-speaking paraprofessional. For part of the day, Kou was placed in an *ESL pull-out program*. Because of this, he often missed the content that was being taught to the mainstream children. Kou hated being pulled out and begged his teachers not to make him leave the rest of his classmates.

Kou developed conversational English fairly rapidly, so school officials decided he no longer needed ESL support. Now in sixth grade, Kou speaks English without a foreign accent, and he appears to understand everything his teachers say. However, Kou never developed literacy in his first language, and his English literacy skills are considerably below grade level. He is a reluctant reader and writer of English, and school officials fear he is getting involved with gangs.

A second example of a long-term English learner is José. He was born in Guadalajara, Mexico, and came to the United States when he was in first grade. José had no preschool or kindergarten in Mexico. In first grade, he was placed in a bilingual classroom. However, after one year, José's family moved to another small farming community where he did not receive first language support. He was mainstreamed for most of the day and pulled out for ESL. In third grade, the family moved again, and José stopped receiving any special services. His family settled in a small city, where his father is a farm worker and his mother is employed in a local fruit-packing plant.

Now, at the end of his freshman year of high school, José can communicate in English and Spanish, but he lacks academic English. He struggles with reading and writing in English and never developed literacy in Spanish. Despite his academic struggles, José is a star on the school's soccer team, which keeps him interested in school.

His high school developmental reading teacher does many things that support students like José. He teaches around relevant themes, provides students with high-interest reading and time to read, and provides strategies to help his students read content area texts. His teacher is optimistic about José, who is trying hard and beginning to see that school is important. However, he is also realistic about José and many of the other long-term English learners in his reading class. He knows they need continued support and encouragement if they are going to pass high school exit exams.

Kou and José represent a third group of students, long-term English learners. These students have been in U.S. schools for seven or more years. Indeed, many are high school students who were born here or began school in the United States. Usually, they have been in and out of various ESL and bilingual classes without ever having received any kind of consistent support program.

These students are below grade level in reading and writing and usually in math as well. Often, they get passing grades, C's and even sometimes B's when they do the required work. Because teachers may be passing them simply because they turn in the work, their grades give many of these students a false perception of their academic achievement. However, when they take standardized tests, their scores are low. Students like Kou and José have conversational fluency in English but lack the academic English and content knowledge they need to compete with native English speakers. Figure 1.1 summarizes the three types of English learners.

Figure 1.1: **Types of English Learners** (adapted from Olsen and Jaramillo, 1999)

Newly arrived with adequate schooling (Stephanie)	• recent arrivals (less than five years in the United States) • adequate schooling in native country • soon catch up academically • may still score low on standardized tests given in English
Newly arrived with limited formal schooling (Guillermo and Osman)	• recent arrivals (less than five years in the United States) • interrupted or limited schooling in native country • limited native language literacy • below grade level in math • poor academic achievement
Long-term English learner (Kou and José)	• seven or more years in the United States • have had ESL or bilingual instruction, but no consistent program • below grade level in reading and writing • mismatch between student perception of achievement and actual grades • some get adequate grades but score low on tests

Cortés' Contextual Interaction Model

Previous schooling and knowledge of English are only two of the factors that affect students' school success. Schools are charged with educating all students. If some students or groups of students fail consistently, an explanation must be found. Cortés (1986) developed a Contextual Interaction Model to illustrate the interplay among factors that influence school success for ELLs. Figure 1.2 is an adaptation of Cortés' model (D. Freeman & Y. Freeman, 2001). As this figure shows, both the community context and the school context contribute to the success or failure of students. At the same time, the kinds of students produced by a school influence the social context because these graduates become key players in their local communities.

Figure 1.2: **Cortés' Contextual Interaction Model**

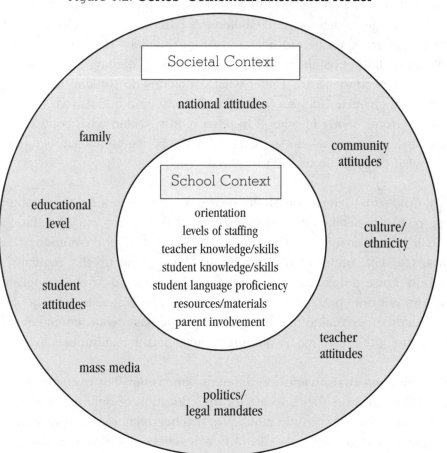

Cortés' model suggests that multiple factors must be taken into account when considering student school achievement. He warns against single-cause explanations. For example, there are some educators who believe that if ELLs were only immersed in all-English instruction, they would succeed in school. Stephanie and Kou, however, both received all-English instruction, but Stephanie succeeded while Kou struggled, so other factors must also have influenced their academic achievement. As Cortés states, "This model rejects single-cause explanations and instead seeks to incorporate a multiplicity of factors that may influence educational achievement" (p. 23).

Cortés points out that educators have often attributed success or failure to single causes because they have confused cause and correlation. Just because two things occur together, one cannot conclude that one causes the other. For example, there are those who believe that lack of parental involvement causes second language students to fail. Guillermo's parents were very concerned about his progress, yet he did not succeed immediately. His parents' involvement did not compensate for other factors. According to Cortés, the question we need to ask is, "Under what conditions do students with similar sociocultural characteristics succeed educationally, and under what conditions do they perform poorly in school? In other words, within what contexts— educational and societal—do students of similar backgrounds succeed, and within what contexts do they do less well?" (p. 17).

Cortés' Contextual Interaction Model provides a framework for answering this question. The societal context includes general community attitudes, families and their educational levels, the culture and ethnicity of the community members, teacher and student attitudes, and legal mandates that regulate education. For example, in California, Massachusetts, and Arizona, English Only laws not only prohibit the use of students' first languages in schools but also reflect the perception that the general public has toward immigrants. Unfortunately, the mass media often reinforces negative attitudes.

The school context also varies on different dimensions. For example, schools differ in the resources they allocate for the education of different student groups. They also differ in the number of teachers that are hired as well as the required background and skills of new teachers. For example, one school might hire teachers with knowledge of how to work effectively with ELLs, while another school might not take this factor into consideration. Schools also make choices about the kinds of materials they purchase and the types of curriculum they implement. The students' own knowledge and skills along with their language proficiency also are part of the school context. Further, the quality of parental involvement shapes the school context.

ELLs who come to St. Paul, for example, find themselves in a supportive community and school context. The community welcomes refugees, and the celebrations of different cultures held throughout the year show this. The interest in and respect for Somali culture has been so strong that the school administration produced a handbook for teachers that is used throughout the district and requested by other districts around the country. Somali students who enter schools in other communities may find themselves in a very different context. In one city in the Northeast, there was so little understanding and acceptance of Somali refugees that the mayor openly called for Somalis to leave the city and look for other places to live, a statement that was published in the newspaper. It would be difficult for a Somali student to do well in that social context.

The Contextual Interaction Model is dynamic. Societal and educational contexts constantly change as new families enter the community and the school. For example, when we visited Minnesota, educators spoke about the impact the large numbers of refugees from Somalia had had on their classrooms and how they had needed to apply different approaches with them than with the Mexican immigrants. At the time of our visit, they were preparing for the next new wave of refugees coming from Tibet and knew these students would bring new challenges.

Cortés' model is a two-way model. The school context is influenced by the larger social context, and the social context is also affected by the attitudes, knowledge, and skills of the students who leave schools and return to the community. Some ELLs who graduate from college abandon their cultural roots and assimilate into the mainstream. Often, they move away from the neighborhoods where they grew up, thus depriving younger members of their home communities of good role models. Other ELLs return to their communities. They change the community, sometimes assuming leadership roles, but, at the same time, their parents and grandparents may feel that they have abandoned traditional values. As a result, educated ELLs may feel conflicted because they are not sure of their own values or identities.

Students' success or failure results from complex interactions of dynamic contexts. The stories above certainly show this. No one factor can explain success or failure by itself, but change in any one area may alter the dynamics of the whole system in such a way that success is more likely. For example, José was influenced by his interest in and skill with playing soccer. It probably led him away from becoming a dropout. This was not the only influence, however. His parents stopped moving and settled in one place, and his teacher used a relevant curriculum with him. This combination of factors increased José's chances of school success.

Curriculum for ELLs

Teachers like José's are part of the complex contextual interaction that influences students' academic achievement. There is a consensus among researchers on the kind of curriculum that helps ELLs. Too often, however, second language learners are placed in classes that don't build the academic concepts and language they lack. G. García (2000), for example, noted that because these students struggle, they are often given basic skills and repetitive drills rather than activities that build the high-level content knowledge, language, and comprehension skills that they need. They often attend schools with limited access to technology, or the technology that is available is used to drill and teach basic rather than higher-order skills. Rarely do teachers use approaches that have been proven to be effective with English learners.

Other researchers have also found that second language learners are not getting the curriculum they need. Berman (1992) conducted research showing that many schools have not implemented the kinds of programs that are effective for struggling English learners. He reports that students are placed in a passive role, classes are organized as age-based groups in which there is tracking, and the curriculum is abstract and driven by standardized tests. The curriculum in less-effective programs usually has little connection to students' lives. In his summary of research on the needs of language minority students, Goldenberg (1996) critiqued classrooms where students are given whole-class instruction and seat work with limited opportunities "to talk, ask and answer questions, read aloud, and otherwise actively engage in learning language and content" (p. 354).

Concerns about appropriate curriculum have been echoed in several different publications. In 2006, Civic Enterprises published a report on interviews with 467 ethnically and racially diverse high school dropouts from around the United States. The major reason students reported for their dropping out was that classes were not interesting. Eighty-one percent of the students said there should be opportunities for real-world and experiential learning, improved instruction, and academic supports (Bridgeland et al., 2006).

The National Clearinghouse for Comprehensive School Reform reported on a forum of ELL and bilingual educators from different regions around the country. The consensus of these experts was that "public education has never fundamentally changed its core policies and practices to more effectively serve and adapt to the needs of culturally and linguistically diverse students" (Housman & Martinez, 2002, p. 2). They agreed that the curriculum for most English language learners lacked academic rigor, and they noted that many ELLs were placed in low tracks. They stated that ELLs need to be challenged and treated like gifted students, and curricula should be based on principles of experiential education and service learning to engage them in real-world learning. In addition, there was a call to support and draw on students' first languages and cultures. However, these experts could cite only a few positive examples of schools or teachers that were implementing these practices. They concluded, "Despite the consensus of the research, policies and practices that implement these principles in any comprehensive way are rare" (p. 2).

Christian (2000) summarized characteristics of programs that address the needs of ELLs. Her conclusions are similar to those reported by other researchers. She stated that there must be high standards for both the language learning and academic achievement of ELLs and instructional personnel who can implement effective instructional strategies including the integration of language and academic content learning. Christian also cited the importance of professional development for specialist teachers and for all teachers who work with second language learners, appropriate curriculum and instructional materials, and program designs that respond to local conditions.

Current research on ELLs suggests that certain practices are most effective in promoting high academic achievement. Although student success will vary depending on a number of factors in their own backgrounds and in the social context and the general school context, individual teachers can still make a significant difference. In the following chapters we explain the practices that have proven most effective in working with ELLs, and we provide examples of teachers at different grade levels who have helped their ELLs succeed.

Conclusion

English language learners are found in schools across the country. In some areas there are large numbers of newcomers, often refugees. In other areas, immigrants have come to seek better economic opportunities. Their children enter school not speaking English, even if they were born here. Sometimes most of the second language learners in a school district are from the same linguistic and cultural background, but in other districts the ELLs come from many different countries. All the students need support to succeed in studying academic content in English, but they come to school with different backgrounds including different educational preparation in their first languages. In order for educators to best serve ELLs, they must first know their students. They should have information about students' first languages, about their previous educational background, and to the extent possible, about their families and family histories.

In addition to knowing their students, teachers should understand the political and cultural context in which their students live and learn. When communities, states, and even the country do not welcome immigrants, this influences how students feel about themselves and their schooling. When teachers understand the struggles that students face both in school and outside of school, they are better able to respond to their students and support them in their learning.

In the following chapters, we explain how teachers can best support English language learners. We discuss the importance of teaching language through content, integrating content studies through relevant themes, supporting students' first languages and cultures, helping students develop reading proficiency, and building academic language. In each chapter, we provide classroom scenarios in which teachers use effective practices to help their English language learners develop both academic English and subject-area knowledge and skills.

Applications for Chapter 1

1. Reflect on the four districts described at the beginning of the chapter. Which district is most like your own? List similarities and differences. If you are not yet teaching, choose a nearby district to compare to those in the chapter. What are some of the challenges that the district faces in meeting the needs of ELLs? How is the district responding to these students?

2. We described three kinds of English learners found in schools: Stephanie represented the new arrivals with adequate formal schooling; Guillermo and Osman represented the students who arrive with limited and/or interrupted schooling; and Kou and José represented long-term ELLs. Interview several ELL students in your school. Determine which type of ELL each student is. Be prepared to describe the students to others in class with details such as those we included in the chapter for Stephanie, Guillermo, Osman, Kou, and José. If you are not yet teaching, visit a classroom with ELL students, obtain permission to interview some ELLs, and bring your results to class.

3. Review Cortés' Contextual Interaction Model. Using one of the students you interviewed for question #2, describe the different factors from the Contextual Interaction Model that seem to affect that student. Be prepared to discuss this in class.

CHAPTER 2

Teach Language Through Content

"At this moment, there are more than 6 billion people on the planet! It's hard to picture so many people at one time—but what if we imagine the whole world as a village of just 100 people? In the global village there are almost 6,000 languages, but more than half of the people speak these 8 languages: 22 speak a Chinese dialect, 9 speak English, 8 speak Hindi, 7 speak Spanish, 4 speak Arabic, 4 speak Bengali, 3 speak Portuguese, 3 speak Russian" (D. J. Smith, 2002, p. 10).

These facts comes from *If the World Were a Village*, a fascinating book that tells readers what percentages of people in the world speak different languages, come from different countries, are different ages, have different levels of education, and own different portions of the world's wealth. The book is an excellent starting place for the development of a content theme in which students learn about geography, economics, science, math, and the social studies concept of interdependence. A study of the world as a global village is particularly relevant to English language learners whose first languages are some of those 6,000 world languages Smith mentions. Through a thematic study about the interdependence of people, animals, and nature around the world, second language learners acquire English as they study academic content.

If the World Were a Village

Francisco teaches third grade to a group of diverse students. He chose the unit on interdependence because he wanted to draw on his students' backgrounds and experiences. About half of his students are English language learners. Most of the ELLs are Latinos, several of whom began school speaking only Spanish.

However, he also has two students whose first language is Punjabi, one student whose first language is Vietnamese, and another whose first language is Arabic. The native speakers of English include several African-American students who add to the rich diversity of his classroom.

Francisco planned his interdependence theme to meet state standards in different content areas. For example, in math, students are expected to learn place value, and they should be able to read a bar graph. In social studies, third-grade students are expected to be able to locate areas on maps and globes. In science, they should understand how the components of a system relate to one another and to the whole. Francisco's daily routine includes a language arts block in the morning. In the afternoon, he teaches social studies, science, math, and enrichment such as music and art. He stresses language development and academic content development for all his students throughout the day.

Francisco introduced the theme with the book *If the World Were a Village* (D. J. Smith, 2002) during shared reading in the language arts block. He showed the students the classroom globe, and they talked about where they or their ancestors had come from. Then Francisco read to the students about how many people are in the world and how many  are in the imaginary, reduced global village. He read sections of the book telling the number of people in the global village who would come from different countries, the languages they would speak, their age ranges, and their religions. After a whole-class discussion of the book, students worked in pairs to write about how the students in their classroom were the same as and different from the people in the global village. Francisco then taught a mini-lesson on capitalization, and the pairs checked their papers to see whether they had capitalized the names of countries and languages as well as religions.

Later that day, during social studies, Francisco read *Somewhere in the Universe* (Drew, 1988) to give students a perspective on how their own community fits into the universe. This book begins with the Milky Way galaxy and moves to our solar system, Earth, the United States, their state, their city, and their neighborhood. The students also read *Our Book of Maps* (2004), which shows how to make different kinds of maps and ends with a discussion of the globe. Students then used the classroom globe to locate the countries they had read about in the morning. They found the countries with the largest populations and those with the largest number of speakers of the world's eight major languages.

Since students were studying place value and learning to count by tens, hundreds, and thousands in math, Francisco read some of the statistics again from *If the World Were a Village* and repeated the figure of 6 billion people living in the world. He then asked students to write out that number and other statistics from the book and identify the place values. In small groups the students also made graphs showing the number of people in the countries with the largest populations.

Over the next few days, to introduce the idea of how everyone in the world has some connection to others, Francisco read aloud several books about children all over the world who, though different in some ways, have similar interests, needs, and goals. These included *Whoever You Are* (Fox, 1997), *This Is the Way We Go to School: A Book About Children Around the World* (Baer, 1990), and, for his Spanish speakers, *Canción de todos los niños del mundo (Song of All the Children of the World)* (Ada, 1993). The class also read *We're All Special* and the Spanish version, *Todos somos especiales* (Maguire, 1999a, 1999b), to discuss the unique gifts each person has.

During language arts, students wrote paragraphs comparing and contrasting themselves with other children in the world. Since the language arts standards include poetry, Francisco read *I Am of Two Places* and *Soy de dos lugares* (Carden & Cappellini, 1997a, 1997b). The Spanish version served as a preview and review for his Spanish speakers. In these books, immigrant children write poems about family traditions and their immigrant experiences. Francisco's students talked about their native countries and traditions or those of their ancestors. Working in small groups, they wrote interview questions to ask family members about their family traditions and immigrant experiences. Students then used the results of the interviews to write their own poems for a class poetry book. Figure 2.1 contains a bibliography of the books Francisco used during this unit.

Figure 2.1: **Interdependence Unit Bibliography**

Ada, A. F. (1993). *Canción de todos los niños del mundo*. Boston: Houghton Mifflin Company.

Baer, E. (1990). *This is the way we go to school: A book about children around the world*. New York: Scholastic.

Carden, M., & Cappellini, M. (1997a). *I am of two places*. Crystal Lake, IL: Rigby.

Carden, M., & Cappellini, M. (1997b). *Soy de dos lugares*. Crystal Lake, IL: Rigby.

Drew, D. (1988). *Somewhere in the universe*. Crystal Lake, IL: Rigby.

Fox, M. (1997). *Whoever you are*. San Diego, CA: Harcourt Brace.

Maguire, A. (1999a). *Todos somos especiales*. León, Spain: Editorial Everest.

Maguire, A. (1999b). *We're all special*. León, Spain: Editorial Everest.

Our book of maps. (2004). Barrington, IL: Rigby.

Smith, D. J. (2002). *If the world were a village*. Toronto: Kids Can Press.

During social studies, students located the native countries of each child's family on a large world map and marked the countries with pushpins. In math they graphed how many students came from each country. They also graphed how many members there were in their families. Francisco used this activity as a bridge to move to the next part of the interdependence unit, the importance of families and how family members help one another.

Francisco's unit provides an example of how to teach language through content to English language learners. Rather than trying to teach English grammar and vocabulary as separate subjects for his ELLs, Francisco engages them in activities that facilitate the acquisition of both academic English and content area knowledge. The approach Francisco takes is a relatively new one in the history of second language teaching.

From Traditional Approaches to Content-Based Language Teaching

Traditional approaches to teaching a second language focused on the grammar and vocabulary of the new language. Students memorized vocabulary lists and studied endings for different verb tenses. Often, the greatest benefit of this approach was that students learned English grammar for the first time. But they seldom learned to understand, speak, read, or write the second language.

In the 1960s, the methodology for teaching a second language shifted from an emphasis on grammar and vocabulary to a concern with communication. Students practiced dialogues and engaged in group activities designed to help them use the new language to talk to classmates. Reading and writing were introduced at more advanced stages. Grammar was seldom studied. Vocabulary was acquired in the process of authentic language use.

The *communicative approach* to language teaching and learning worked quite well. Students learned to interact with others in a new language. Lessons gradually introduced different aspects of the second language. For example, early lessons might involve students in using the present tense, and later lessons would require the past tense as students talked about what they did the previous week. Students were not explicitly taught that they were using a past-tense form of the verb. Rather, they acquired additional aspects of the language through use.

For people who want to visit another country and communicate in the language used there, the communicative approach works well. However, English language learners generally pick up English outside school, on the playground, or by watching TV. Because they live in an English-speaking environment, they acquire the language that is all around them. Newly arrived ELLs benefit from some instruction in school to supplement this natural acquisition process. Since most students gain basic communicative competence in a new language fairly quickly, ESL programs for newcomers can be of fairly short duration.

Although ELLs soon acquire enough English to interact with their peers and to understand their teacher's directions ("Take your seat and open your science book to page 20"), they still lack the academic language of the different subject areas. ELLs who develop conversational English but lack academic English struggle in school. After all, tests in science, social studies, math, or language arts use academic English, not basic communicative skills in English.

The recognition that ELLs soon gain the ability to communicate in English but lack academic English proficiency led ESL teachers to shift from a focus on basic communication to teaching English through the different academic content areas. The movement for *content-based language teaching* began at the university level and gradually filtered down to the lower grades. At the same time, the responsibility for teaching ELLs also shifted. ESL specialists might work with newcomers, but in many areas of the country, every teacher is expected to help ELLs in their class learn both English and the grade-level academic content. As the number of ELLs continues to grow, there is an increased need for teachers everywhere to attend to both language and content as they teach.

Content-based language teaching is based on a theory of second language acquisition that claims we acquire rather than learn a new language. In this chapter, we first outline this theory. Then, we explain different approaches that have been developed for teaching language through content. Next, we discuss four reasons to teach ELLs language through content. We conclude by describing a second unit to show how effective teachers can teach all their students both language and content.

Krashen's Theory of Second Language Acquisition

Krashen (2003) used the term *learning* to refer to a conscious process of language development that occurs as a result of direct teaching. In contrast, *acquisition* is a subconscious process of language development that occurs as the result of exposure to meaningful messages in a language. Even though some researchers have argued that there is a continuum moving from acquisition to learning rather than a clear distinction, the two terms are widely used in the research literature, and the distinction seems to be a useful one.

Most researchers agree that many aspects of a child's first language are acquired. Children seem to acquire the phonology of a language. Within a fairly short time, they can understand and produce messages in a language their parents or other caregivers use to communicate with them. In addition to the sounds of the language, children acquire the syntax. Experiments with very young children reared by English-speaking parents show that they understand the difference between "Big Bird is washing Cookie Monster" and "Cookie Monster is washing Big Bird." This research demonstrates that children recognize that there is a link between the order of the words and the meaning and that in English, the first noun phrase is the subject or actor while the second is the object of the sentence.

First Language Acquisition

Support for the claim that first languages are acquired, not learned, comes from Chomsky's (1965) theories of linguistics. Chomsky, the foremost linguist in the United States, developed a theory referred to as *generative linguistics*. Chomsky was interested in describing language in terms of a set of rules that could be applied to generate all the sentences of a particular language. Since there is no limit on the number of different sentences that can be expressed in any language, there must be a finite set of rules capable of generating an infinite number of sentences. For this description to reflect psychological reality, the number of rules must be relatively small. Otherwise, humans couldn't acquire them.

Chomsky's answer to the question of how children acquire language is that children have an innate capacity for language, which he first called a *language acquisition device* (LAD). The LAD is a specialized area of the brain designed for language. According to Chomsky, humans do not simply have a special cognitive capacity for figuring out language. Rather, humans are born with the basic structures of all human languages already present in the brain. Chomsky calls this innate knowledge of language *Universal Grammar* (UG). Children are not born with knowledge of English or Japanese or any other human language. Instead, they are born with knowledge of those elements that are common to all human languages.

As a result, the task facing children is not to learn how language works, starting from scratch. Instead, since children are born with an implicit knowledge of language in general, they have to figure out how the particular language (or languages) they hear functions. For example, all languages have something like prepositions, words that show relationships among things

("The book is on the table"). In languages like English these words that show position come in front of the noun, so they are called *prepositions*. In other languages, these words follow the noun, so in those languages, a child would encounter sentences with the pattern ("The book is the table on"). In such languages, these words are called *postpositions* because they come after (post), not before (pre).

Children are born with the built-in knowledge that the language they hear will have a word to show position. What children must figure out is whether the position word precedes the noun or follows it. This is a much easier task than starting without any knowledge and having to learn that there are some words that show position and also having to learn where those words go in the sentence. If children have a Universal Grammar, this hard-wired knowledge, then it is not surprising that most children acquire the language that surrounds them. Not all of language is innate. Certainly, children have to learn individual words. Vocabulary can't be built in because it is not completely systematic and predictable. There is no regular connection between the sounds of words and their meanings. Even though there are patterns within vocabulary that enable children (and adults) to develop vocabulary knowledge fairly rapidly, learning vocabulary is different from acquiring the phonology or syntax of a language. However, Chomsky's claim is that most of language is innate. He and other linguists base this claim on certain facts: (1) most children acquire a first language rapidly and without formal instruction, (2) they do this with only a limited amount of evidence, and (3) they do it with only limited feedback.

Second Language Acquisition

Krashen bases his theory of second language acquisition on Chomsky's theory of linguistics. Krashen claims that the same process that enables a child to acquire a first language applies to a child or an adult acquiring a second language. Evidence for Krashen's position comes from the fact that most students who attempt to learn a second language in school fail to reach high levels of proficiency and quickly lose their ability to speak the language if they do not continue to use it. On the other hand, people who live in an area where communication takes place in a second language seem to be able to pick up the language naturally and to retain it. In this context, the second language is acquired, not learned. In addition to his *acquisition/learning hypothesis*, Krashen developed several other hypotheses to account for how second languages are acquired. These include the Natural Order Hypothesis, the Monitor Hypothesis, the Input Hypothesis, and the Affective Filter Hypothesis.

The Natural Order Hypothesis

Krashen reviews research that shows that language, both first language and second language, is acquired in a natural order. Simply put, some aspects of language appear in the speech of language learners before other features. For example, babies acquiring English first produce sounds with vowels (usually the low, back-placed *ah* sound) and later add consonants beginning with consonants formed with the lips, such as *p* or *m*. This helps explain why the first word of many infants is something like *mama* or *papa*, much to the delight of a parent. Sounds such as *r* come later. That's why young children might say, like Elmer Fudd, *wabbit* instead of *rabbit*. Other parts of language also appear in a natural order. Statements come before questions. Positive statements come before negatives, and so on.

Researchers in second language have found the same phenomenon. The natural order of second language acquisition differs slightly from that of first language, but there is a definite order. Dulay and Burt (1974) studied Spanish and Chinese speakers acquiring English. They looked at the order in which certain morphemes appeared. They noted that the plural *s* in a word like *toys* showed up in children's speech earlier than the third person *s* of present-tense verbs in sentences like "He plays." Whether researchers look at the acquisition of sounds, word parts, or sentence patterns, they find an order of acquisition for English that is the same even for children whose first languages are different. The order seems to come from the language being acquired, not a transfer of features from the first language.

The Monitor Hypothesis

This hypothesis helps explain the role of learning in the process of language acquisition. The phonology, morphology, and syntax of a language are acquired. Acquisition is what enables native English speakers to tell what "sounds right" in the language. They may not be able to explain why "He is married to her" sounds better than "He is married with her," but because native speakers have acquired the language, they can make these kinds of judgments.

Learned knowledge also plays a role in language competence. The rules that people learn can be used to monitor spoken or written output. In other words, people can use these rules to check what they say or write. In order for monitor use to be effective, language users must have time, they must focus on language form, and they must know the rules. Even in the first language, most people monitor their speech in formal situations, such as giving a speech to a large group of people. To use the monitor effectively, one must have learned the rules. Is it *different from* or *different than*? Unless the speaker has learned the right answer, he or she can't monitor the output very well.

Spoken language is difficult to monitor using learned rules because if speakers start focusing on form, they cannot focus on meaning at the same time. However, editing during the writing process represents an ideal situation to apply the monitor because there is time, and writers can focus specifically on the correctness of the language—learned knowledge—to be sure that sentences are complete and words are spelled correctly. On the other hand, when writers are drafting, they may depend more on their acquired knowledge because too much focus on form may interrupt the flow of their ideas.

The Input Hypothesis

How does acquisition take place? According to Krashen, the key is *comprehensible input*—messages, either oral or written, that students understand. Not all input leads to acquisition. Krashen says that students acquire language when they receive input that is slightly beyond their current level. He refers to this as $i + 1$ (input plus one). If students receive input that is below or at their current level $(i + 0)$, there is nothing new to acquire. However, if the input is too much beyond their current level $(i + 10$, for example), it is not comprehensible.

Providing comprehensible input is not an exact science. Teachers can't possibly ensure that everything they say or write will be exactly at the $i + 1$

level for every student. The students in a class are all at different levels of proficiency. Nevertheless, as long as students understand most of what they hear or read in a new language, they will acquire the language. Different students will acquire different parts of the language depending on their current level. Krashen (2004) is an especially strong advocate of reading for language acquisition. He cites research showing that reading provides excellent comprehensible input and is the source of one's knowledge of vocabulary, grammar, and spelling.

The Affective Filter Hypothesis

How do affective factors such as nervousness, boredom, or anxiety influence language acquisition? If language is acquired when a person receives comprehensible input, that input has to reach the part of the brain that processes language (LAD). Boredom or anxiety are affective factors that can serve as a kind of filter to block out incoming messages and prevent them from reaching the LAD. As a result, even though a teacher may present a very comprehensible lesson, some students may not acquire the language of the presentation because their affective filter operates to block the input. Students cannot acquire language that never reaches the LAD. On the other hand, when the filter is open, when students are relaxed and engaged in a lesson, even messages that are not easy to comprehend will trigger the acquisition process.

Krashen's theory of second language acquisition claims that second languages are acquired, not learned. The process is the same as for first language acquisition. Acquisition occurs in a natural order when people receive comprehensible input and their affective filter is low. Rules that people learn can be used to monitor the output, either speech or writing. Krashen's theory of second language acquisition provides the theoretical base for content-based language teaching.

Content-Based Language Teaching

If ELLs can acquire English by getting comprehensible input—messages they understand—in English, then those messages could be about science or literature rather than everyday topics like clothes or food. Content-based language teaching is designed to provide ELLs with comprehensible academic content in English. The idea is that ELLs can acquire English as they learn their academic subjects. Over time, different methods for teaching language through content have been developed.

Krashen and Terrell (1983) proposed the *Natural Approach*, a content-based method of teaching ESL applied most often at the elementary level. Teachers used various techniques to make instruction comprehensible as they taught lessons on topics such as families, animals, or nutrition. Student use of English was mainly oral until learners reached an intermediate level of proficiency. While the Natural Approach was widely used in elementary grades, educators in the upper grades found the content demand for their subjects was greater, and students needed to be able to read and write as well as respond orally to instruction. An added problem was that mainstream teachers at the upper grades and at the secondary level generally used fewer techniques designed to make lessons understandable for ELLs.

A program model for older students proposed by Krashen (1985) included a component called *sheltered content*. In this model, students are taught some subjects in their primary language, some in sheltered classes, and some in mainstream classes. As students become more proficient, they are transitioned from primary language instruction to sheltered instruction, and then they are mainstreamed. For example, students might take social studies classes at first in their primary language. Later, they would have a sheltered social studies class, and eventually they would be mainstreamed in social studies.

ELLs were grouped for placement in sheltered classes. The classes were sheltered in two respects. First, ELLs were sheltered because they didn't have to compete with native English speakers. Second, the content was sheltered since the teachers used techniques to make the English instruction more comprehensible. Sheltered instruction was a step in the right direction because in these classes students were instructed in content area subjects, and they acquired English at the same time. Figure 2.2 lists techniques teachers in sheltered classes can use to make the content more comprehensible for students with limited English proficiency.

Figure 2.2: **Strategies to Make the Input Comprehensible**

1. Draw on students' first languages to preview and review the lesson.
2. Use visuals and realia (real things). Always try to move from the concrete to the abstract.
3. Scaffold content learning through the use of graphic organizers, including Venn diagrams, webs, and charts.
4. Use gestures and body language.
5. Speak clearly and pause often, but don't slow down speech unnaturally.
6. Say the same thing in different ways (paraphrase).
7. Write down key words and ideas. (This slows down the language.)
8. Use media, PowerPoint, overheads, and charts whenever appropriate.
9. Make frequent comprehension checks.
10. Above all, keep oral presentations or reading assignments short. Collaborative activities are more effective than lectures or assigned readings.

Three problems arose with sheltered instruction. The first was that teachers were often not adequately prepared to teach ELL. A high school biology teacher, for example, might be given a two- or three-hour in-service on sheltered techniques and then be expected to work effectively with English learners. This was simply not enough time. The second problem was that content teachers were forced to slow down in order to make lessons understandable for second language students. As a result, teachers of sheltered classes were seldom able to cover as much content as mainstream teachers. In effect, academic content was sacrificed to meet language needs.

This led naturally to a third problem. Students who succeeded in sheltered classes often floundered when mainstreamed. They were generally behind in the content, and they had difficulty catching up because the mainstream teacher didn't use the techniques that the English learners still needed. In fact, the real problem with sheltering ELLs may have been separating them from native speakers of English. Even though it is easier to teach students who are grouped by language proficiency, there are benefits when ELLs interact with native English speakers in an academic-content classroom. The native speakers provide models of good speaking and writing that ELLs need.

In other words, separating ELLs is more convenient, but it is not the best approach. Instead, teachers need to be able to differentiate instruction to meet the needs of students with different levels of English proficiency as well as different levels of academic background in each subject area.

Developing academic English proficiency takes time. Studies by Cummins (2000) and Collier (1989) have shown that academic language development takes from four to nine years. These findings are based on student scores on standardized tests of reading in English. Even middle-class ELLs whose parents are college-educated need on the average at least four years to score at the 50th percentile on nationally normed tests given in English. For that reason, it is not surprising that ELLs who moved from sheltered to mainstream classes struggled academically. They still needed continued support to develop the English proficiency necessary for learning in the different content area subjects.

The Cognitive Academic Language Learning Approach (CALLA)

Chamot and O'Malley (1989) developed the *Cognitive Academic Language Learning Approach* (CALLA) as a useful guide for teachers implementing sheltered English. CALLA is a cognitive model of learning designed to help ELLs become active learners who focus on concepts and meanings rather than language forms. Teachers in CALLA classes deliver grade-appropriate content and work to help ELLs develop academic language. They also emphasize metacognitive strategies. ELLs learn and apply specific strategies as they study academic content.

CALLA teachers develop five-phase lesson plans that include preparation, presentation, practice, evaluation, and expansion. During the preparation stage, students engage in activities designed to activate background knowledge. For example, a lesson on the water cycle might begin with a review of the different forms water takes. Next, teachers present new information, using different techniques to ensure that the input is comprehensible. A teacher might read a short picture book that shows the different stages of the water cycle and explains each stage.

In the third phase of a CALLA lesson, students practice talking and writing about the concept being presented. Often, during the practice, students work in cooperative groups. They might illustrate and label each stage of the water cycle. The practice is the major part of the lesson. Practice is followed by evaluation. CALLA emphasizes student self-evaluation. Students are asked to review the main vocabulary and concepts from the lesson and check to see how well they understood each one. CALLA lessons end with expansion activities during which students make connections between the new knowledge that has been presented and what they learned in previous lessons.

Chamot and O'Malley wrote many sample lessons in the different content areas to give teachers concrete examples of how to develop effective lessons for ELLs. The approach was very helpful for many teachers of sheltered classes. However, some teachers found it difficult to make their own plans following the CALLA model because this was a new approach that required extra work. In addition, even with well-designed lessons, ELLs who are at lower levels of English proficiency and those who lack background knowledge struggle to learn grade-appropriate content in English.

A New Approach: ELD and SDAIE

The failure of ELLs to succeed in mainstream classes after sheltered instruction caused educators to rethink the goals of content-based ESL. Was the goal content or was it language? Should students in a sheltered biology class be learning English through studying biology, or should they be learning biology through the medium of English? Often, ELLs with different levels of English proficiency and different degrees of subject-area knowledge were grouped in the same sheltered class. Students with relatively low levels of English proficiency could not learn as much biology as their classmates with greater English proficiency. In addition, students with limited science background could not understand more advanced science instruction.

In California, a state with many ELLs, two different types of classes were developed to replace the earlier approach of placing a mixture of ELLs in sheltered classes. Instead, ELLs at the beginning or early intermediate stages of English acquisition are placed in English language development (ELD) classes. These classes can be taught by either ESL teachers or mainstream teachers who have received additional training in working with ELLs.

In ELD classes, teachers teach the regular school subjects. As they teach math, science, social studies, or language arts, they focus on developing the academic language the ELLs need to understand, talk, read, and write about each content area. Students are tested on their English proficiency rather than on their knowledge of specific subject areas. ELLs get both academic content and academic English, but the emphasis is on English language development. ELD classes are appropriate for students with limited formal schooling and for ELLs with adequate formal schooling who are still in early stages of English language acquisition.

For ELLs with more advanced levels of English proficiency and at least some background in the subject areas, a second type of class was developed. These students are placed in *Specially Designed Academic Instruction in English* (SDAIE) classes. In these classes, teachers make accommodations for students' limited English proficiency as they teach the different academic subjects. Often, they cover fewer topics in greater depth. ELLs in SDAIE classes are tested on their knowledge of the academic subjects, not on their English proficiency. SDAIE teachers recognize that ELLs, even at the advanced stages, still make certain kinds of errors in speaking or writing. For example, they might have difficulty with two-word verbs such as *refer to,* or their writing might reflect patterns from their first language.

Other states, following California's lead, have started to implement ELD and SDAIE classes. The development of ELD and SDAIE classes solves many of the problems associated with sheltered English. Both ELD and SDAIE classes offer content-based instruction for ELLs. The distinction between the two kinds of classes reflects an awareness of important differences among ELLs. By offering two kinds of classes, schools can meet the needs of ELLs at different stages of English acquisition and with different levels of academic background. Figure 2.3 contrasts ELD and SDAIE.

Figure 2.3: **ELD and SDAIE**

Student Characteristics

ELD	SDAIE
English proficiency—beginner or low intermediate	English proficiency—high intermediate to advanced
L1 academic proficiency—not considered	L1 academic proficiency—at or near grade level

Focus of Instruction and Evaluation

ELD	SDAIE
Teach language through content with emphasis on language development	Teach grade-appropriate content using special techniques to make the language understandable
Evaluation focuses on language	Evaluation focuses on academic content

The Sheltered Instruction Observation Protocol (SIOP) Model

Content-based language teaching has gone through a number of refinements. From sheltered language teaching, through CALLA and ELD/SDAIE, this model has been tested and improved. Although it takes several years for ELLs to perform academically on the same level as their native English-speaking peers, good content-based language instruction can facilitate the process of acquiring academic English and subject-matter knowledge.

One of the best-researched and most highly developed models is the *Sheltered Instruction Observation Protocol* (SIOP) model. The SIOP is a checklist that can be used to determine whether or not all the elements of effective instruction are present in a lesson. This tool helps administrators or researchers evaluate how well research-based practices are being implemented in a classroom. Observers using the protocol rate each of these items on a five-point scale. Teachers can refer to the checklist as they plan lessons for their ELLs. The SIOP is comprehensive, and it reflects the best current knowledge on how to help ELLs learn both subject-matter content and academic English.

The checklist contains 30 items grouped into three main sections: preparation, instruction, and review/assessment. Preparation includes lesson planning and the selection of materials. In some cases, materials need to be adapted or supplemented. An important part of the preparation phase is the development of content and language objectives. These are drawn from state standards since ELLs need to meet the same standards as all other students.

Since teachers in content-based language classes teach language through content, they need to have two kinds of objectives. *Content objectives* specify what students should know (declarative knowledge) and what they should be able to do to demonstrate understanding of the content (procedural knowledge). For example, a content objective for ELLs studying the water cycle might be to understand the four stages of the water cycle. They would demonstrate this understanding by drawing pictures of the four stages and labeling the pictures.

In addition to content objectives, teachers develop *language objectives*. These objectives specify the language students will use as they learn about particular content. Language objectives can be designed for the text level, sentence level, or word level. A text-level language objective for ELLs studying the water cycle could be to write a science report, one of the genres common to science. We discuss language objectives in more detail in Chapter 6 when we explain academic language.

Content area teachers are accustomed to writing and teaching content objectives. ESL teachers are used to writing and teaching language objectives. A mainstream teacher with ELLs in her class should develop and teach both content and language objectives. This is a real challenge and is an important feature of the preparation section of the SIOP model.

The biggest section of the SIOP protocol is instruction. There are six categories under instruction: building background, comprehensible input, strategies, interactions, practice/application, and lesson delivery. As they plan and teach lessons, effective teachers build background students need for a lesson and make connections between the students' prior experiences and the current lesson. They also plan specific ways to make the input comprehensible, such as using graphic organizers and emphasizing key vocabulary. Teachers also consider different grouping options they will use during a lesson. They might begin with heterogeneous groups and then have students work in pairs, or students with the same language background might be grouped together for certain activities. Teachers carefully plan how they will present the lesson, including the activities in which the students will engage. They also review the kinds of reading and writing students will be doing.

The last section of the SIOP protocol addresses review and assessment. Teachers should review key vocabulary and content concepts. They should assess whether students have learned the content and provide feedback to the students to keep them aware of their progress. A good SIOP lesson would be rated high on all three sections of the protocol: preparation, instruction, and review/assessment. Teachers need extensive training to implement SIOP. They also need time to develop lesson plans that respond to the items on the checklist. They need to adjust the lessons to students' language proficiency and academic preparation. However, the results in schools that have successfully implemented SIOP have been positive. The SIOP protocol reflects the key elements for teaching language through content.

Reasons to Teach Language Through Content

In this chapter, we have discussed Krashen's theory of second language acquisition. This theory holds that people acquire a second language when they receive comprehensible input—messages they understand. ELLs need to develop English proficiency and academic knowledge and skills. If they receive comprehensible input about school subjects, they can accomplish both tasks. Krashen's hypotheses form the theoretical bases for teaching language through content.

We have also briefly traced the development of second language teaching. In traditional ESL classes, the focus was on basic vocabulary and grammar. Then the focus of the instruction shifts to helping students develop basic communicative skills along with knowledge of the new culture. However, basic communicative skills and cultural knowledge are not enough. ELLs also need content knowledge and academic English, so most ESL teachers now provide content-based language instruction.

The content-based approach evolved from early sheltered classes. CALLA helped teachers understand the important elements of content-based language teaching. The distinction between ELD and SDAIE helped schools better place ELLs and focus the sheltered instruction in the areas students most needed. SIOP provides a thorough checklist for planning lessons for ELLs. Many regular classroom teachers have incorporated content-based language teaching to meet the needs of their second language students.

There are four reasons that teaching language through content is important for ELLs. Figure 2.4 lists these reasons.

Figure 2.4: **Reasons to Teach Language Through Content**

In the first place, when teachers teach language through content, students learn both language and content at the same time. There is no need, and indeed, there is no time to teach language first and content later. In classes in which teachers focus on both language structures and forms as they teach literature, science, social studies, or math, ELLs acquire academic English as they learn subject-area content. In the earlier stages of language development, teachers need to use more techniques to make the English instruction comprehensible, so the amount of content that can be taught must necessarily be reduced. As students gain increased English proficiency, they can learn more content in English. Nevertheless, at every stage of language development, ELLs should also be learning academic content. Developing high levels of academic English and academic content proficiency takes time, so it is important that ELLs learn English and subject-matter knowledge from the start.

1. Students get both language and content.

2. Language is kept in its natural context.

3. Students have reasons to use language for real purposes.

4. Students learn the academic vocabulary of the content area.

A second reason for teaching language through content is that this approach keeps language in its natural context. It is natural to talk about the hypotenuse of a triangle if you are studying geometry. Math is the natural context for this word. As they learn this word, students understand how it is related to other words such as *triangle*. It is easier to learn words in context than in isolation or as part of a list of unrelated words. Key words for different subject areas are best understood as part of a network of related terms needed to understand some aspect of a subject. In the area of literature, for example, it is easier to learn a term such as *rising action* in the process of talking about the development of plot. The student comes to understand rising action as one phase of plot development that is related to other words, such as *climax* or *falling action*. Content-based language teaching naturally lends itself to presenting vocabulary in context.

A third reason for teaching language through content is that students have reasons to use the language they are learning. They are not just memorizing words for a test, words they will forget very soon. Instead, they need to use the words as they listen to lectures, talk with classmates, read textbooks, and write reports. Use of vocabulary leads to deeper learning and greater retention. An ELL studying geometry will develop a better understanding of *hypotenuse* as she listens to the teacher explain the parts of a triangle, reads proofs in her textbook, and then engages in problem-solving activities. An ELL studying literature will come to understand *rising action* as he writes an analysis of the plot development in a novel. In each case, the students are motivated to learn the English they need to talk, read, and write about academic content.

A final, related reason for teaching language through content is that students learn the academic vocabulary and text structures of the different content areas. As the previous examples show, students learn key words like *hypotenuse* or *rising action* in the process of listening, reading, talking, and writing about academic subjects. Students also come to understand that in different contexts, the same word takes on different meanings. In math, students learn their multiplication tables. In chemistry, they might study the periodic table. In geology, they encounter the water table. And as they study different subject areas, they consult a table of contents. They also learn to gather information from charts and tables. Studying a word like *table* as part of a list would never prepare a student to learn the different meanings of the term as it is used in different content areas.

Students learn more than academic vocabulary as they learn language through content. They also learn the forms of writing used in different academic fields. We discuss academic language in more detail in Chapter 6. Academic language includes knowledge of the different genres of writing used in different academic disciplines. For example, a history report is different from a personal narrative. ELLs begin to learn these differences as they read and write in the different content areas. They also learn to use language for different functions, such as to describe, explain, or persuade. The only way that ELLs can develop the academic language they need for school success is to be immersed in that language as they study the different content areas. In the following section we provide another example of a teacher who successfully teaches language through content.

Veronica's Unit on Insects

" Itsy Bitsy Spider went up the water spout. Down came the rain and washed the spider out..." (Trapani, 1996). These are the beginning lines of the well-known song about spiders that many native English-speaking preschoolers and kindergarteners sing inside and outside school across the country. However, the children enthusiastically singing this song in Veronica's kindergarten class were not all native English speakers. In fact, only about half of her students came to school this fall speaking English fluently. Her students speak several different first languages including Spanish, Vietnamese, Khmer, Arabic, and several Indian languages including Urdu and Punjabi.

Veronica has been teaching in her urban district for five years, and she has found that each year more students enter her classroom as English language learners. Because of this, she has taken some university coursework toward certification in ESL and has learned about the best ways to reach the new students. One of the most effective ways she has found to help them acquire English and learn the kindergarten curriculum is teaching them language through content.

As she plans units of study, Veronica makes sure that she also meets the state content area standards. In science, kindergarten students are expected to ask questions, gather information, and communicate their findings. In addition, they should be able to identify the properties of organisms. During this unit, Veronica planned to teach her students about the differences between spiders and insects by having them notice that spiders have eight legs while insects have only six. In language arts, kindergarten students are expected to develop their oral language vocabulary. They also should learn to identify letters of the alphabet and match letters and sounds in words. Veronica planned different activities to help her students develop important beginning reading skills.

Songs are especially effective for teaching reading, and Veronica and her students also sang a counting song about elephants balancing on a spider web, "One Elephant, Two Elephants" (Wainman, 1982). She wrote the words on large song sheets and clipped the songs to her song chart. The children sang the songs together as a student volunteer tracked the words. Veronica also asked the Spanish speakers if they knew the song in Spanish, "Los elefantes" (Ada, 1991), which is similar to the elephant song in English but has a different tune. Since some students were familiar with the song in Spanish, Veronica put those words up on the song sheet, too, and the whole class sang it in Spanish led by the Spanish speakers and accompanied by a tape.

Veronica then asked the students what the songs had in common. The children immediately called out, "Spiders." Next, Veronica asked the students what they knew about spiders and wrote down student responses: "They are bugs." "They can bite you." "I don't like spiders." "They eat flies." "They make webs." "Baby spiders come from eggs." After they had discussed spiders, Veronica read *The Very Busy Spider* (Carle, 1984). All the students wanted to feel the raised spider web on each page, so Veronica allowed one student to come up each time a page was turned. The children talked about the spider web catching the fly at the end of the story. When they talked about spiders and flies, Veronica asked them what the two had in common. "They are bugs!" several children replied. For the next day, Veronica asked the students to try to find a bug and bring it in a jar with twigs and leaves. She suggested that the students ask for help from their parents to be sure none of the children would get stung or bitten.

The next day, several students brought in bugs to show. Some had beetles; some had ants; others had caterpillars or crickets. One student brought in a moth, one had a butterfly, two had ladybugs, and one had a bee. First, Veronica read to them *Have You Seen Bugs?* (Oppenheim, 1996), a delightful rhyming book about bugs. The book explains where bugs are found, what they eat, and how they reproduce.

Veronica asked the students to think about where they found their bugs and if their bugs were like the ones discussed in the book. During share time, the children showed their bugs to their classmates and told them how and where they had caught them. Many of the children connected their experience to the book Veronica had just read. On a large strip of paper, Veronica wrote the name of the bug each child had found. She and the students talked about the first letter of the words and the different sounds they heard. For example, Veronica explained, "*Bee* has the same first sound as *beetle*. Do you notice any other words that have the same first sound as *B* in *bee* and *beetle*?"

Veronica placed all the jars of bugs on a table at the front of the classroom, and laid out strips of paper with the bug names next to the jars. Next, she read three limited-text books from a science series for emergent readers: *Bugs, Bugs, Bugs,* (Reid & Chessen, 1998), *Where Do Insects Live?* (Canizares & Reid, 1993), and *What Do Insects Do?* (Canizares & Chanko, 1998). These books are illustrated with large photographs of insects. The children were fascinated by the pictures and commented on the bugs they recognized. Since the text is limited and predictable, Veronica encouraged students to read along with her. Then she invited the students to read the books with her a second time so everyone could think about the pictures, the words, and the information in the books.

Next, each child was asked to choose a bug to draw and write about. Veronica told the children that to get ideas for their drawing and writing they could look at the bugs in the jars or use the books she had read or other books about insects she had in the room. She pointed out that she had several books in Spanish including one about ladybugs, *La mariquita* (Cappellini, 1993); one about flies, *La mosca* (Almada, 1993b); and another about mosquitoes, *El mosquito* (Almada, 1993a). Veronica showed the children the pictures in the books and told them they could all look at those pictures and that maybe some Spanish speaker could help them if they wanted to read the books.

As the students began their work, Veronica encouraged her three Spanish speakers to listen to *Insectos asombrosos* (*Amazing Insects*) (Kite, 1997) and was pleased when four other students in the class, including two Southeast Asian children, also came to listen. For the Spanish speakers, this short book reinforced concepts already discussed, such as where insects live and how they eat. The non-Spanish speakers contributed to the reading by asking questions about the pictures.

As the children drew their bugs and labeled their pictures or wrote short sentences about their insects, they made important observations. Some students noticed that spiders have eight legs, but beetles, ants, bees, and butterflies have only six. Veronica put up large posters of an insect and a spider and discussed with all the children the difference in number of legs.

The next day, Veronica began by inviting children to share their pictures and what they had written on their drawings. Students hung their pictures around the room under letters of the alphabet; so ants were under *A*, and caterpillars and crickets were hung under *C*. Then Veronica took out the word strips she had made the day before and asked students to pin the large printed words under the letter of the alphabet the word started with. When the students were finished, their pictures and the large printed insect words covered the walls under letters of the alphabet.

At recess that day, several children had trouble finding their insects in the jars among the twigs and leaves. This brought up the concept of camouflage, so after lunch Veronica read *How to Hide a Butterfly and Other Insects* (Heller, 1985) and *The Big Bug Search* (Jackson, 1998), books that show how insects are camouflaged in nature. The children loved finding the insects in the illustrations of leaves and branches. Next, Veronica brought out an old favorite, *The Very Hungry Caterpillar* (Carle, 1969). First, she did a *picture walk* with the book. She turned the pages and had students tell her what they saw and what they thought was happening. Picture walks help ELLs build vocabulary and help all students focus on the overall meaning of a story before they begin to read. Then the whole class read the book together.

After reading the book, the children talked about how a caterpillar changes into a butterfly. Veronica took out a new story, *La mariposa* (*The Butterfly*) (F. Jiménez, 1998). She read the English version of the book (which has a Spanish title). It tells the story of a first-grade Hispanic boy who does not speak English. He is lonely at school. His only joy comes from watching a caterpillar in the classroom spin a cocoon and eventually emerge as a beautiful butterfly. During the discussion that followed, many of the children in the class related to the loneliness of the non-English speaker. Veronica then showed the class a caterpillar that she had brought in a jar. She explained that they would watch the caterpillar change into a butterfly over the next few weeks, just as Francisco did in the story.

Another butterfly book that Veronica showed the students was *The Butterfly Alphabet* (Sandved, 1996). The author took photographs of butterflies all over the world. By taking close-ups of butterfly wings, he was able to include patterns that represented each of the letters in the alphabet. As she read the poetry on each page, Veronica showed the class the page, and they identified the alphabet letter on the wing. During free reading time that day, Veronica put out a variety of books for students to read, including the camouflage books and *The Butterfly Alphabet Book*. She also displayed *The Butterfly Counting Book* (Pallotta, 1998) and some limited-text books such as *Butterfly* (Canizares, 1998) and *The Tiny Dot* (Whitney, 1996) for students to read together and discuss. As she moved around the room, she was excited to see how involved all her students were in reading and discussing the books. Figure 2.5 lists the books Veronica used in her unit on insects.

Because her students speak several different languages, Veronica teaches mainly in English. She is able to preview lessons in Spanish when working in small groups with her Spanish-speaking students, and she has gathered some resources in Spanish. However, she has few resources in Vietnamese, Khmer, or the Indian languages of her other bilingual students. Her unit on bugs is an example of how she carefully chooses activities and materials that help her students develop academic concepts and academic English.

Figure 2.5: **Insect Unit Bibliography**

Ada, A. F. (1991). *Días y días de poesía*. Carmel, CA: Hampton-Brown.

Almada, P. (1993a). *El mosquito*. Crystal Lake, IL: Rigby.

Almada, P. (1993b). *La mosca*. Crystal Lake, IL: Rigby.

Canizares, S. (1998). *Butterfly*. New York: Scholastic.

Canizares, S., & Chanko, P. (1998). *What do insects do?* New York: Scholastic.

Canizares, S., & Reid, M. (1993). *Where do insects live?* New York: Scholastic.

Cappellini, M. (1993). *La mariquita*. Crystal Lake, IL: Rigby.

Carle, E. (1969). *The very hungry caterpillar*. Cleveland, OH: The World Publishing Company.

Carle, E. (1984). *The very busy spider*. New York: Scholastic.

Heller, R. (1985). *How to hide a butterfly and other insects*. New York: Grosset and Dunlap.

Jackson, I. (1998). *The big bug search*. New York: Scholastic.

Jiménez, F. (1998). *La mariposa*. Boston: Houghton Mifflin.

Kite, P. (1997). *Insectos asombrosos*. Boston: Houghton Mifflin.

Oppenheim, J. (1996). *Have you seen bugs?* New York: Scholastic.

Pallotta, J. (1998). *The butterfly counting book*. New York: Scholastic.

Reid, M., & Chessen, B. (1998). *Bugs, bugs, bugs*. New York: Scholastic.

Sandved, K. B. (1996). *The butterfly alphabet*. New York: Scholastic.

Trapani, I. (1996). *The itsy bitsy spider*. Boston: Houghton Mifflin.

Wainman, M. (1982). *One elephant, two elephants*. Port Coquitlam, Canada: Class Size Books.

Whitney, N. (1996). *The tiny dot*. Boston: Houghton Mifflin.

Conclusion

In this chapter we have given a brief overview of second language teaching methods. Content-based language teaching is based on a theory of second language acquisition that holds that we acquire a second language when we receive comprehensible input in that language. If that input is focused on academic content, then students can acquire English, and they can develop the knowledge and skills of the different content areas at the same time. Francisco and Veronica, whose units of study we have described here, teach language through content to all their students, including their second language learners, because they realize the importance of helping all their students develop academic English and content area knowledge. In the following chapter, we provide further examples of successful teaching as we explain why teachers should organize their curriculum around meaningful themes based on big questions.

Applications for Chapter 2

1. If you studied a second language in school, think back on how you were taught that language. Did you study the language traditionally, learning grammar and vocabulary? Was the emphasis more on talking about everyday events? Have you used the second language outside of the classroom? Can you still speak and understand the language today? Be prepared to talk about your language learning experience and connect it to the approaches discussed in the chapter.

2. Review Krashen's hypotheses including the learning/acquisition hypothesis, the natural order hypothesis, the monitor hypothesis, the input hypothesis, and the affective filter hypothesis. Explain each hypothesis in your own words and connect each to a language learning experience of your own or to what you have observed with ELLs in schools.

3. Plan a lesson for a class that includes ELLs. Incorporate at least four of the "Strategies to Make the Input Comprehensible" listed in the chapter (page 44).

4. We discussed several content-based approaches to teaching, including the Natural Approach CALLA, sheltered instruction, ELD, SDAIE, and SIOP. Do you see any of these being used in your school or in a school you visit? What is your evaluation of the effectiveness of the approach?

5. Francisco and Veronica taught language through content with their units on interdependence and insects. Find examples in the units that show how teaching language through content helped students learn both language and content at the same time. How did teaching language through content help students develop academic language? How was language kept in its natural context? Be specific.

CHAPTER 3

Organize Curriculum Around Themes

Organizing curriculum around themes is beneficial for all students. However, it is especially important that teachers working with ELLs organize their curriculum thematically. We begin this chapter by showing how a third-grade teacher organizes his curriculum around themes. Then we consider different ways to organize curriculum. We explain six reasons that organizing around themes benefits ELLs. We conclude with an example of effective thematic instruction with ELLs at the secondary level.

Daniel's Ocean Theme

Daniel teaches third grade in a rural farming community. Up to third grade, Spanish-speaking students in the district receive much of their daily content and literacy instruction in Spanish, although they also have daily ESL classes. Beginning in third grade, most instruction is given in English. The ELLs in Daniel's class have some conversational English but lack academic English. Daniel knows that all his students will be tested in third grade for reading proficiency in English. There is a large block of time dedicated to language arts each day, but Daniel worries that students also need to develop content knowledge in science and social studies, which will be tested as students move into the upper grades. To help his students with literacy and content, Daniel uses lots of reading and writing during science and social studies lessons to help his students develop literacy as they learn content.

A good example of Daniel's teaching is an ocean unit he developed drawing on third-grade science standards, which call for understanding diverse life forms in different environments including the ocean. The standards also ask that students know that living things cause changes in the environment, and those changes are both beneficial and detrimental.

Because Daniel's students come from a rural, agricultural area, and many have had little previous experience with the sea, he decided to start his unit by giving them time to think about and talk informally about the ocean and its inhabitants. Daniel first brought out the world globe and asked the students to notice how much of the globe is covered by water. Together the class listed the names of the oceans and estimated what percent of the Earth is water. He read to them some pages from *Water All Around the Earth* (Weil, 2004), which explains that water covers between 70 to 75 percent of the Earth's surface. The students and Daniel discussed how important the oceans are since they make up so much of the planet. One of the big questions, then, that the class decided to investigate was, "What is in the ocean?"

The following day, Daniel continued the ocean study by drawing on the strengths of the Spanish speakers in his class. He asked them to take turns reading the pages of a big book about what is in the ocean, *En aguas profundas* (*In the Depths*) (García-Moliner, 1993). These students then summarized each page in English for the non-Spanish readers in the class.

Next, Daniel took out a big book in English, *The Mighty Ocean* (Berger, 1996), and did a picture walk with the class. Daniel asked students to look at the pictures in the big book and comment to one another quietly on what they saw as he turned the pages. He also asked his ELLs to think about what things they saw there that they could talk about in English. Once they finished looking at the book, students dictated in English words and phrases about the ocean that the book had brought to mind.

Then Daniel read the book to them, stopping to answer their questions and to discuss parts that especially piqued their interest. As he turned each page, he asked students what they saw on the pages. Since *The Mighty Ocean* repeated many of the concepts that the students had already read about in *En aguas profundas*, Daniel led the students in a comparison of the two books using a Venn diagram. In this way, both concepts and vocabulary about the ocean were reinforced.

To continue to help his ELLs develop academic English and content area knowledge, Daniel divided the students into heterogeneous groups, including students who were more proficient and students who were less proficient readers of English in each group. He gave the groups books about the ocean at different levels of difficulty. These included *Under the Ocean* (Bennett, 1999), *In the Deep* (2004), *Ocean Life* (Leonhardt, 2000), *In the Ocean* (Wachter, 2004), *Big Animals in the Sea* (Windsor, 1999a), *Sea Lights* (Rice, 2001), and *On the Seashore* (Windsor, 1999b).

He asked the students to read the books together and make a list of what they had learned about the ocean. As groups finished their lists, they went up to a large piece of butcher paper in the front of the room that had the title "What do we know about the ocean?" and wrote what they knew, including the names of animals and plants and areas where animals lived in the ocean, as well as facts, such as some sea animals live in the dark and have their own lights, and some sea animals and plants are endangered.

Daniel put up another piece of paper and wrote, "What do you want to learn?" then asked students to tell him what more they wanted to learn related to the ocean. This question led students to ask questions about different sea animals, especially dolphins, whales, and sharks.

During the next few days, Daniel and his students read many additional books and magazines about the ocean. In the *Kids Discover* magazine, *Oceans* (Sands, 1997), they found a chart of ocean animals and plants living at different depths that paralleled charts found in both *En aguas profundas* and *The Mighty Ocean*. Daniel read aloud *A Day Under Water* (Kovacs, 1987), and the class talked about how scientists travel near the floor of the ocean and how they study the animals and plants there. Figure 3.1 lists the books Daniel used during the ocean unit.

Daniel and his students were interested in shells of animals that live near or in the ocean. Daniel brought in shells he had collected. His students examined the shells and identified them by using the resource books in the classroom.

As they read and talked, the students began using the academic English vocabulary of the content area.

Daniel divided his class into groups to study different sea animals. Each group chose an animal that they became the experts on. Many students were interested in sharks, dolphins, and whales, but other students wanted to know about smaller fish, lobsters, crabs, and octopuses. One group got interested in coral and coral reefs. Using the Internet, students collected information on their animal and wrote reports that they illustrated. Each group presented their findings to their classmates using their drawings and pictures they had collected. A key concern that came out of these reports was how both ocean animals and plants were endangered. Another big question that resulted was, "How can we save our oceans?"

After learning so much about the ocean, the students did several culminating activities. They made a class mural showing the seashore and the ocean at different depths. Using construction paper, they made different sea animals and plants based on information contained in the reports they had written earlier, the Internet, and the resources around the room. The students worked together to place their creations on the mural. Working in their groups, they typed on the computer a short description of their section of the mural, printed it in large letters, and placed it next to the mural.

Figure 3.1: **Ocean Unit Bibliography**

Bennett, P. (1999). *Under the ocean*. New York: Scholastic.

Berger, M. (1996). *The mighty ocean*. New York: Newbridge Communications Inc.

García-Moliner, G. (1993). *En aguas profundas*. Boston: Hougton Mifflin.

In the deep. (2004). Barrington, IL: Rigby.

Kovacs, D. (1987). *A day under water*. New York: Scholastic.

Leonhardt, A. (2000). *Ocean life: Tide pool creatures*. Austin, TX: Steck-Vaughn.

Rice, H. (2001). *Sea lights*. Katonah, NY: Richard C. Owen.

Sands, S. (1997). *Oceans*. New York: Kids Discover.

Wachter, J. (2004). *In the ocean*. Barrington, IL: Rigby.

Weil, A. (2004). *Water all around the earth*. Barrington, IL: Rigby.

Windsor, J. (1999a). *Big animals in the sea*. Crystal Lake, IL: Rigby.

Windsor, J. (1999b). *On the seashore*. Crystal Lake, IL: Rigby.

The final project was an individually designed poster about the ocean. The students could choose to draw and write anything they wanted on their poster, but most students chose to write about taking care of the ocean. The walls of Daniel's room were covered with posters including "Save the Whales," "Don't Throw Garbage Into the Ocean," "We Need to Take Care of the Ocean or We Are Going to Die," and "Save the Ocean. It's the Home of the Fish."

Students in Daniel's class learned a great deal during their study of the ocean. Daniel's students learned important science content related to state standards, and they developed their academic English. By teaching language through content organized around a theme, Daniel helped his ELLs make the transition into English.

Ways to Organize Curriculum

Schools organize curriculum in different ways. In some schools or classes, the subjects are not connected. In other settings, subjects are linked through a common topic, such as apples or spiders. A third way to organize curriculum is to organize themes around big questions and then use resources from each subject area to investigate the theme. It is this third, inquiry-based approach that we advocate. In the following sections, we examine each of these ways of organizing curriculum.

The Cha-Cha-Cha Curriculum

In some classes we have observed, each subject is treated separately. Within a particular subject, there may be thematic organization. For example, in language arts, students might be engaged in a unit on exploration. The reading selections and writing activities all relate to this theme. However, the theme of exploration is not carried through into science, social studies, or math.

Students who are studying exploration in language arts might be learning about cell structures in science, solving problems with one variable in algebra, and reading about state history in social studies. As the teacher shifts content areas, students have to start thinking about totally different topics. Donald Graves has termed this way of organizing the *cha-cha-cha* curriculum.

Students might begin the day by reading a story about arctic exploration, and then—*cha-cha-cha*—they switch to cell structures in science. When science study ends—*cha-cha-cha*—it's time to think about algebra problems. From algebra, students *cha-cha-cha* to state history. Each subject may have internal consistency, but many ELLs get lost in the transition from one content area to the next. Just when they fully understand that the language arts lesson is about exploration, the teacher moves on to cell structures in science. It takes second language students a few minutes to understand that this is a lesson about cell structures. Each time the teacher changes to a new content area, ELLs have a period during which they are not sure what topic is being studied. They cannot afford to lose this valuable time.

The *cha-cha-cha* curriculum may occur in an elementary class with a single teacher teaching all the subjects. It is more prevalent in intermediate grades because there is more departmentalization. When different teachers teach each subject, it is more difficult to coordinate curriculum, although it can be done. At middle school and high school, the difficulty of organizing curriculum around themes increases due to scheduling difficulties. Even though some middle schools and high schools have successfully implemented thematic curriculum, they are exceptions.

The *cha-cha-cha* curriculum offers the least support for ELLs, and, in fact, it is not effective for any student. Because there are no links between content areas, students do not revisit ideas. Once language arts is over, they do not have to focus on exploration again until the next day. What they learn is compartmentalized. In addition, the vocabulary they are developing as they study exploration does not naturally recur in any of the other subjects, so there is less chance for students to acquire the academic vocabulary they need to succeed. A good approach to curriculum should, at least, link the content areas and help students come to view school as an integrated whole rather than as a series of discrete topics to be studied for a short time each day and then shelved until the next day.

The Gummy Bear Curriculum

A step toward more connected thematic organization is the attempt to unite different subject areas around a common topic. Kucer and Silva (2006) describe this way of curriculum organization as the gummy bear curriculum. They give the example of a theme organized around bears. The teacher has decided to use *Ira Sleeps Over* (Waber, 1972) as a central text during the unit of study. This is the story of a young boy who is invited to stay at a friend's house overnight. Despite his sister's teasing, he takes his teddy bear with him for security. The story is about how children use some object for comfort and security. Waber could have chosen to have Ira take a favorite blanket or some other toy. He just happened to choose the teddy bear.

However, a teacher moving toward thematic teaching might focus on the bear as a way to unify the curriculum. After all, there is a bear in the language arts story. During science, the class would study about how bears hibernate. In social studies, they could read about how Teddy Roosevelt spared a bear cub, thus creating the teddy bear. In music, students could sing a song about bears, and in art they could draw pictures of bears. Finally, during math, the students might engage in a hands-on project that involves the counting and manipulation of gummy bear candies.

Although attempting to unify the curriculum in this way is a step in the right direction, there are several problems with this approach. In the first place, some of the bear connections are tenuous at best. A creative teacher might find a way to include bears in every subject, but the result is only a superficial unity. *Ira Sleeps Over* is not a story about bears. ELLs might recognize the bear element in each subject, but when the teacher moves from language arts to science or any of the other content areas, ELLs would still be lost. In social studies they would be learning about a particular politician, and in math the lesson would be on counting, adding, or subtracting. There is no fundamental connection between a story about a boy who needs some object to feel secure in a new situation and a science reading about how and why bears hibernate.

The problem with the gummy bear approach to curriculum design is that bears, spiders, or apples are only surface-level objects. The real point of each lesson has little to do with bears. Students should learn about hibernation, and it happens that bears, as well as other animals, hibernate. An English learner might think she comprehends the lesson because she knows it is about bears, but unless she understands hibernation, she has missed the point. If the teacher is basing lessons on state and federal standards, those standards ask for an understanding of important concepts. Knowing what a bear is would not be listed in the standards. Perhaps the biggest problem with the gummy bear curriculum, though, is that a teacher really has to stretch to connect some subjects to an object like a bear.

It is unlikely that the gummy bear approach would be used at middle or high school. We have seen it only in self-contained classes. Once students begin to move to a different teacher for each subject, there are seldom links across the subject areas. A particular unit in one subject area might have a unifying theme. For example, a language arts teacher could teach a theme on courage. The language arts teacher might collaborate with the social studies teacher on a theme such as courage. But there is less chance of courage being the theme in science or math. Generally, in the upper grades, each teacher follows his or her curriculum without too much concern for what the students are studying in the other content areas.

Curriculum Organized Around Big Questions

A better way to organize curriculum is to explore big questions such as, "How does food get from the field to the table?" or "How does the weather affect our lives?" Wiggins and McTighe (2000) argue that curriculum must deal with big ideas or questions worth investigating. These are questions that do not have a simple answer. During a theme such as "How does food get from the field to the table?" students would use literature and information from the different content areas to build their understanding of plants and plant growth and transportation of products from the farm to the store. The theme might also include smart shopping and healthful eating. Students could use information from language arts, social studies, science, and math as they explore these related topics. Organizing around big questions leads to an inquiry approach to education (Short et al., 1996).

Teachers can connect curriculum to state and federal standards by basing the big questions on these standards. For example, a first-grade science standard is to recognize ways that animals' appearance changes as they mature. Often, grade-one teachers include a unit on growth and change. Turning the topic of growth into a question such as, "How do people and animals change as they grow?" helps focus the curriculum and connects it directly to the standard. This is a big question because it is complex and multifaceted. Students can investigate different aspects of growth and change. The theme also naturally leads into a study of life cycles.

To take another example, a fourth-grade social studies standard requires that students understand the impact of environment on culture. This standard can also be turned into a big question, "How does where we live influence how we live?" Students can begin by studying the local community and then look at other communities that are different from theirs because of differences in the physical environment. A similar standard for secondary students studying world geography is to understand how geographic contexts and processes of spatial exchange influenced events in the past and helped to shape the present. Many standards, like this one, are recycled at higher grade levels so that students can build a deeper understanding of key concepts. At both fourth grade and tenth grade, though, students can approach the ideas through a focused big question.

Teachers can often include literacy, literature, and math standards within questions based on social studies and science standards. It is important to spend time focusing on literacy and math skills, but they are best learned in the context of literature, social studies, and science. For example, students could read a novel or an expository text about weather and climate change during the unit on "How does where we live influence how we live?" They could record the high and low temperatures daily and then graph the results. Both literacy and math skills could be developed as students read and write about this big question.

Basing big questions on standards makes good sense in a time when accountability is being stressed in schools. This approach also is logical because textbooks and supplementary materials available at each grade level reflect the standards. Third-grade students in most states study the solar system, and fourth graders study the rain forest. Teachers at each grade level can meet to plan curriculum together, deciding on the big questions and the materials and methods they will use to engage students in inquiry of these questions. This sort of horizontal planning is also useful because different teachers at the same grade level can teach the theme at different times during the year. This avoids the problem of two or three teachers attempting to use the same resources at the same time. There might be only one or two good solar system charts available, so it is better if each third-grade class studies the solar system at a different time.

At the secondary level, teachers from different subject areas can meet to form interdisciplinary teams. At one large middle school, each team is made up of a language arts teacher, a social studies teacher, a science teacher, and a math teacher. Students rotate through these teachers' classes. This model has resulted in great improvement in the academic performance of the ELLs at the school (D. Freeman & Y. Freeman, 2001). Some high schools have also organized the curriculum around big questions that draw on the different subject areas (E. García, 2002). Organizing interdisciplinary units at the secondary level is complex, but the results have been consistently positive. In schools that do not take this approach, teachers either organize their own curriculum around themes or pair up with a teacher from another content area to plan a theme. For example, the math teacher might coordinate with the science teacher.

Benefits of Organizing Curriculum Around Big Question Themes

Organizing curriculum around themes is beneficial for all students. However, this approach is particularly important for ELLs for several reasons. Figure 3.2 lists six benefits of organizing curriculum around big question themes.

In the first place, the thematic focus provides a context within which students can better understand instruction in a second language. In the same way that it is easier to assemble a jigsaw puzzle if we can look at the picture on the cover, it is easier for students to make sense of individual lessons when they know the topic. Students engaged in the study of a question such as, "How do animals

Figure 3.2: **Benefits of Organizing Curriculum Around Big Question Themes**

1. Since students see the big picture, the English instruction is more comprehensible.

2. Content areas (math, science, social studies, language arts) are interrelated.

3. Vocabulary is repeated naturally as it appears in different content area studies.

4. Because the curriculum makes sense, second language students are more fully engaged and experience more success.

5. Teachers can differentiate instruction to accommodate differences in language proficiency.

6. Through themes, teachers can connect curriculum to students' lives and backgrounds.

and people change as they grow?" know that each lesson will relate to this topic. Since ELLs have the big picture, they can make better sense of a math lesson in which they compare the growth rate of two animals or of a science lesson in which they study the stages of growth from a tadpole to a frog.

A second benefit of organizing around themes is that teachers can help students make connections across subject areas. Students investigating a big question such as, "How does where we live affect how we live?" might learn about the conditions that cause hurricanes during science, locate areas where hurricanes have struck during geography, and read a story about a family whose home was devastated by a hurricane in language arts. In math, students could study charts showing changes in wind velocity as hurricanes travel across water and chart these changes. They could study how meteorologists use data to predict the course of a hurricane. Knowledge gained in one subject area can be used in studying another area. Teachers can also remind students of what they learned during math or science as they read a story or write a report in language arts.

When subject areas are interrelated through the focus on a central theme, students keep thinking and learning about the big question as they move from subject to subject or class to class. What they learn in math may be applied in social studies or science. They can't simply put math out of their minds once the math lesson is over. The more that subjects are interrelated, the greater the chance that a second language learner will understand the instruction. What the students don't fully comprehend during science might become clear when the topic is revisited during social studies or language arts.

Maintaining the same topic through the focus on a big question also ensures that key vocabulary will be repeated naturally in the different subject areas. In the past, ESL teachers used repetition to help students learn vocabulary. A teacher would have the class or a student repeat a word or phrase as a way of improving pronunciation and memorizing the words. However, second language acquisition research has shown that we do not learn a new language through imitation and repetition. The problem with repetition is that it can become mindless, much like writing out each spelling word ten times. To acquire some aspect of language, such as a word or phrase, students need to encounter it several times in meaningful contexts. By organizing around themes, teachers provide the repeated exposure to meaningful language that students need. Rather than hearing a word like *temperature* only in science class, an ELL might hear or see it again during language arts, social studies, and math. Since the subjects are interrelated, some of the same vocabulary comes up in each subject area, and this increases a student's chance of acquiring important academic vocabulary.

Listening to someone speak a language we do not understand well is mentally tiring. Our brains naturally attend to things that make sense, so if a reading passage or a lecture is hard to understand, our attention turns to something else, something we can understand. For this reason, it is critical that teachers do everything possible to make instruction comprehensible for ELLs. One way to do this is to organize around themes. Even when students don't fully understand the language of a new lesson, they know it is connected to the theme, and they stay engaged for a longer period of time. It is this engagement that leads to both language development and increased subject-matter knowledge. If ELLs can stay focused on the lesson being delivered in English, there is a greater chance that they will learn the concepts and acquire more of the new language. The result is more success in writing papers, presenting reports, or taking a quiz on the subject. And success increases motivation to make that mental effort needed to comprehend new subjects in a new language. Thematic organization makes curriculum more comprehensible, and this leads to more sustained engagement and greater success.

A fifth benefit of organizing around themes is that teachers can more easily differentiate instruction to meet the needs of ELLs at different levels of English proficiency. Even when teachers have only three or four ELLs in a class, these students may be at quite different proficiency levels. One might be a beginner while another is at the intermediate level, and two more are advanced. As long as all the students are studying the same theme, teachers can adjust assignments to suit the varied proficiency levels of the students. For example, during the theme based on the question "How does food get from the field to the table?" the beginning student might read a picture book that shows how the fruit, juice, milk, cereal, and toast some Americans eat for breakfast get from the farm to the store. This student could represent his understanding by drawing and labeling pictures of each step. Intermediate and advanced students could read more challenging books on the topic and demonstrate their understanding by making a complex chart or writing a paragraph to explain how food gets from the field to the table.

Themes based on big questions are universal. Animals and people everywhere change and grow. The weather affects our lives no matter where we live. Since the curriculum focuses on such big questions, teachers can connect subject-area studies with students' lives. In fact, ELLs can often make important contributions to a class by giving examples from countries where they or their parents have lived. Some students in the United States might eat cereal, toast, and juice for breakfast, while a student from Vietnam might have rice and fish. Both students can draw on their own background experience as they learn how food gets from the field to the table. At the same time, the variety of examples coming from a class with students from different backgrounds expands the curriculum and enriches the learning experience for all the students.

Organizing curriculum around big questions provides these six benefits for ELLs. Instruction is more comprehensible, the subject areas are interrelated, vocabulary is repeated naturally, students stay more engaged, and teachers can differentiate instruction and connect curriculum to students' lives. In the section that follows, we describe how one secondary teacher organized curriculum around a big question to provide these benefits to her students.

Mary's Sense-of-Self Unit

The high school where Mary teaches has a large Hispanic population as well as a sizable group of students whose first language is Punjabi. The school schedule is organized into four block classes per day. Students take eight classes, so they see their teachers every other day. Teachers teach seven classes and have one preparation period every other day. The block schedule provides extended time for students to read, write, and talk together about significant themes.

Mary teaches one beginning ESL class of newcomers, a second-year ESL class, and regular ninth-grade English classes that include both native English speakers and long-term English learners. Since Mary has so many different classes, she needs to plan in such a way that she meets the standards for her grade level, challenges her students academically, and provides them with ample time for reading and writing activities. She needs to do this without becoming completely overwhelmed in her planning. Therefore, she organizes all her classes around the same basic theme, offering all her students the same kinds of challenging activities while still adjusting instruction to meet the varying language levels of her different classes.

Developing a Sense of Self

Mary created a unit she called "Developing a Sense of Self" to help her high school students answer the big question, "Who am I?" She knew students needed to learn to appreciate the diversity in their school and their world. In order to do this, they needed to better understand themselves. Mary based her unit on the state language arts writing standards that called for students to write biographical and autobiographical narratives, to relate a sequence of events and communicate the significance of the events, to locate scenes and incidents in specific places, and to make use of descriptions of appearance, images, and sensory details.

Her theme study, taught at the beginning of the year, served other important purposes: It helped Mary's students set goals, and it helped Mary get to know her students. As her students set goals and talked and wrote about themselves and classmates, Mary gained insight into their lives. In addition, the students got to know one another. Mary found her students enjoyed this theme because the activities focused on them.

The first activity that Mary asked the students to do was to think about three goals for her class. Mary and the students talked about what goals were, and they brainstormed together what some appropriate goals might be. For each goal, students filled out a sheet answering the questions, "What do you need to do to reach this goal?" and "Who can help you?" At the bottom of the sheet, students answered one last question: "What have you done so far this year that relates to your goals?"

José, one of Mary's new ELLs, listed his three goals as "finish school," "learnd more english," and "be a nice people." He listed "do my homework," "pay attention," and "come to school" as some of the things he needed to do to accomplish his goals. For the question about what he had done so far, he wrote, "I do my homework. started to work hard and be myself."

After the students completed their goals sheets, Mary had them work in pairs to interview each other. Mary gave them the following questions as an interview guide:

- What is your name?
- Where were you born?
- How many brothers and sisters do you have?
- What do you do for fun?
- What is your favorite sport? Favorite team?
- What is your favorite food?
- What is your favorite book?
- What is your favorite movie and/or TV show?
- When you think of English class, what do you think of?
- What are your plans for the future?
- What is something interesting or unique about you?

The students wrote down their partner's answers and then used them to introduce their partner to the class.

Once students had set goals and started to learn about their classmates, Mary organized activities to help them think about how they were like others and yet were unique. One activity that helped students think about themselves and value their individuality was making a coat of arms. Students drew an empty coat of arms with five sections to fill in. In each section, they drew a picture that revealed something about themselves. For example, one section was to show "something you do well," another "your greatest success," another "some special place you like to be," another "your favorite musical group," and still another "your dream for your future." After students finished drawing their personal coats of arms, they shared them in pairs. The students showed their coat of arms to their partner and asked the partner to guess what the drawings represented. Then they explained each drawing. After this, students worked in groups to make a cumulative coat of arms that they shared with the whole class.

Some students in Mary's ESL 1 classes simply drew pictures and others cut out pictures and labeled them. These pictures represented student responses to slightly modified questions and included "things I love to do," "my favorite book," "what I want to do in the future," "where I want to live in the future," and "what I like to eat." Students with more English proficiency also drew but they wrote more in each section rather than simply labeling them. This coat-of-arms activity provided a scaffold for students, giving them opportunities to use language as they shared how they were the same as or different from their peers. It also provided the background and built vocabulary for other activities requiring more reading and writing in English.

Figure 3.3: **"I Am"**

I am (*two characteristics you have*)
I wonder (*something you are curious about*)
I hear (*something you often hear*)
I see (*something/someone you see regularly*)
I want
I am (*repeat first line*)

I pretend
I feel (*an emotion you feel sometimes*)
I worry
I cry (*something that makes you sad*)
I am (*repeat first line of poem*)

I believe
I dream
I try
I hope
I am (*repeat first line of poem*)

Mary followed these introductory projects with a series of other, related activities. To help her students prepare to write an autobiographical piece, Mary introduced two activities—"I Am" and Autobiopoem. Each activity was designed to help students expand their vocabulary by describing sensory details and images. The "I Am" activity asks students to write a poem by completing sentences about themselves (see Figure 3.3). Students need to put only one or two words to complete each line. For example, the first line has the words "I am" and directs the writer to add two of their characteristics.

An extension that builds on this "I Am" poem is "Autobiopoem" (see Figure 3.4). Students write another poem that includes more details about themselves than the first one. On the second line, for instance, students are asked to list four of their traits. Mary used a template that a colleague gave her. Several other templates are available on various Web sites.

Mary found that her students enjoyed writing and illustrating both their "I Am" poems and their Autobiopoems. Although students in her ESL classes had some difficulty understanding all the categories, and their English was not always perfect, they did an

Figure 3.4: **Autobiopoem**

Follow the directions, and you will discover that you are a poet. Write only what is indicated on each line.

Line 1: *Your first name*

Line 2: *Four traits (adjectives) that describe you*

Line 3: Son/daughter of… *or* Brother/sister of…

Line 4: Who loves (*3 people, ideas, or a combination*)

Line 5: Who feels (*3 sensations*)

Line 6: Who finds happiness in (*3 items*)

Line 7: Who needs (*3 items*)

Line 8: Who gives (*3 items*)

Line 9: Who fears (*3 items*)

Line 10: Who would like to see (*3 items*)

Line 11: Who enjoys (*3 items*)

Line 12: Who likes to wear (*3 colors or items*)

Line 13: Resident of (*your city, street, or road name*)

Line 14: *Your last name*

excellent job of describing themselves, their wants, and their interests. They were engaged in these projects and wanted to know the English words to describe themselves. They also learned new vocabulary from one another as they shared their poems.

In order to scaffold the writing of longer prose pieces, Mary next asked her students to conduct another interview. In this case, as they worked in pairs they filled out a form called "Here's Looking at You" (see Figure 3.5), which includes questions that ask for more details about students' lives.

Mary's English language learners found this activity much more challenging than the previous ones. To help her students succeed, Mary first talked with her students about the questions to be sure they understood them. Then she had them work in small groups to talk about how they would answer their questions. Finally, she told them that instead of five adjectives, they could write two or three for now. Then students worked in pairs to conduct the interviews and write down the answers. After this, Mary asked them to write two paragraphs about themselves using the information from the "I Am," coat-of-arms, the Autobiopoem, and the "Here's Looking at You"

Figure 3.5: **Here's Looking at You**

1. What five words would you use to describe yourself to me?

2. What five words would your mother (father, teacher) use to describe you?

3. How do teachers see you (include one who likes you and one who does not, if applicable)?

4. What five words would you use to describe school? Tell me about your experiences in school.

5. Tell me about your friends. What do you do together? Where do you go?

6. In school, what are some of your strongest abilities?

7. Out of school, what are your strongest abilities?

8. Which classes are your favorites? What types of activities do you enjoy?

9. What abilities do your parents admire most about you?

10. Describe how you get along with others at school and at home.

11. If you had a chance to be part of a group or to be an individual, which would you choose and why?

12. What is your greatest accomplishment at this time?

activities. Even Mary's beginning ESL students could write something about themselves, a task that would not have been possible without the earlier activities.

Areli wrote the following, which has some errors but certainly gets her messages across:

> *My name is Areli Alonso. I am very happy and romantic. My mother says that I am beauty and responsable. I have a lot of friends but my best friends name is Carmen. My other importants friends are my mother and my sister. My ability out of school is to be friendly. My parents tell me I am intelligent.*
>
> *In school I have the ability of understand easy. I like my school because the people are very kind. My favorite classes are Biology, Geography and sometimes English. I want to learn this year too much.*

Mary teaches her students to edit their writing. With her ELLs she asks them to edit only one or two items for each piece they write. Mary's English learners gain confidence in their ability to write when they can produce extended text after a very short time in the United States. Mary's native English speakers and more advanced ESL students, of course, also benefit from these kinds of activities. Their paragraphs are full of rich details that they drew from previous activities. All her students were able not only to write paragraphs using new vocabulary but also to develop a sense of self through speaking and writing in English.

Conclusion

Organizing curriculum around themes supports ELLs as they learn English and also learn academic content in English. Daniel helped his students develop academic concepts and language through his content theme on oceans. Mary helped her students develop key vocabulary they could use in writing about themselves. Themes help students make sense of the instruction. Another way to help students make sense of instruction is to draw on students' first languages and cultures. In the following chapter, we explain the importance of developing students' first languages, and we provide strategies for supporting students' first languages even when teachers do not speak those languages. We conclude with specific ways to bring students' cultures into the classroom through the use of culturally relevant texts.

Applications for Chapter 3

1. Think about units of study or themes that you have taught or seen taught. Would they fit best under the gummy bear curriculum, or were they organized around big questions? Be specific as you discuss how the theme fits into one of the two approaches.

2. Reread the sections describing the themes that Daniel and Mary taught. Look at Figure 3.2: Benefits of Organizing Curriculum Around Big Question Themes (page 70). Choose one of the two themes and find specific activities in the themes that exemplify the benefits for ELLs.

3. Review the standards for your grade level or a grade level you might teach. List some big questions that might serve to organize thematic study related to the standards. Explain how different content areas can be integrated under the big questions and list some activities that students would do during the theme unit to answer the big questions.

CHAPTER 4

Draw on Students' Primary Languages and Cultures

Wood Land • Farm Land

Wet Land • Dry Land

Rough Land • Smooth Land

Low Land • High Land

The above contrasts are found on the first eight pages of the beautifully illustrated book *America: My Land, Your Land, Our Land* (Nikola-Lisa, 1997). Fourteen different artists, representing the rich ethnic diversity of America, illustrate the pages of this unusual book. It offers a wealth of opportunities for teachers working with English language learners to develop language and concepts through meaningful and relevant content. Materials such as the Nikola-Lisa book are particularly useful because they can be adapted for use with students of different ages and at different levels of English proficiency.

Ms. Tolland, an eighth-grade social studies teacher, teaches in a large middle school in a small city in the Central Valley of California. The majority of her students are Latinos, although she also has some Anglo students and some who are Cambodian, Hmong, Filipino, and Laotian. Many of her students are native English speakers, some are long-term English learners who started kindergarten speaking a language other than English, and others are relative newcomers, students just mainstreamed this year. Most of her students struggle to read and understand the adopted textbooks. Writing coherently in English is especially difficult for these students. Ms. Tolland's challenge, then, is to teach the state's grade-eight content standards related to U.S. history and geography to her diverse students. She knows that she needs to differentiate instruction without watering down content and to engage her eighth graders, who do not all see the relevance of studying history and geography.

To begin, Ms. Tolland explains that the book *America: My Land, Your Land, Our Land* is the work of American artists who are from different ethnic and cultural backgrounds, just like the students in her classes. She reads about the artists who are Native American, African American, and of Philippine, Korean, Japanese, Cambodian, and Dominican descent. The artists produced two-page spreads in different art mediums to illustrate the diversity of the United States and the contrasts they saw within the country. Ms. Tolland then reads the very limited-text book, showing students the beautiful art on the two-page spreads.

Next, she asks the students to form small groups and encourages students who speak the same first language to be in the same group. In each of her classes, Ms. Tolland has some native English-speaking groups and several groups of Spanish speakers with one or two groups of speakers of other languages. Students are asked to first choose one of the two-page spreads as a group. Ms. Tolland then gives them a color photocopy of the pages and asks them to discuss several questions: What do you see in the picture? What kinds of emotions do the pieces of art make you feel? Why do you think the artist chose those contrasts? What do the two contrasting pictures tell you about America? Ms. Tolland tells the students they may use their first language to discuss these questions, but they should report back to the class in English.

As one recently mainstreamed group of Spanish-speaking newcomers looked at the art of the first two pages—"Wood Land" and "Farm Land"—they discussed the questions animatedly because one of the pictures shows farm workers walking through a vineyard, picking grapes in the hot sun, something all the students and their parents had experienced. The contrasting picture shows a nearby forest with many trees chopped down. When they reported back in English to Ms. Tolland, their vocabulary was somewhat limited, but it was obvious that they understood key ideas. They listed words like *rows*, *leaves*, *grapes*, *farmers*, *woman*, *basket*, *hot*, and *hard work* as well as *trees*, *cut*, and *sad*. Ms. Tolland wrote these words on the board and asked the students to describe each picture in a sentence, using the words they had generated. The teacher wrote the sentences on chart paper. As she wrote, she arranged the sentences so that contrasting features were made parallel:

> *The wood land has green trees, but many are cut.*
> *The farm land has grapes, but the people work too hard.*

Then she and her students read the sentences together. For homework, she asked the students to draw pictures of farms or wooded places they had lived in or visited and to be ready to talk and write about them.

As she worked with her less-proficient students, her more advanced ELLs as well as her native English speakers worked together in small groups doing a similar activity. They chose a two-page spread and discussed the contrasting pictures. Then they worked together to write a paragraph highlighting the differences between their two pictures. One group wrote about the "wet land" with fish and birds and lots of green plants contrasted with the "dry land" that is devoid of plants and animals because of the pollution of the factories and the cement roads everywhere. One Filipino-speaking group chose the picture of the immigrant grandfather talking about the home country while the child pictures the different lifestyles in the new and old countries. Their paragraph in English contrasted life in the Philippines and life in California.

The following day, Ms. Tolland capitalized on the work students had done the previous day. She used their writing about the contrasting pictures to start a discussion related to one of the important social studies standards: the changing social and political conditions in the United States as a result of the Industrial Revolution, including the effects of urbanization, immigration, and different labor movements. The community where Ms. Tolland teaches was affected by the United Farm Workers' strikes in the past, and Ms. Tolland wanted to help her students understand the importance of these social studies concepts by connecting them to the experiences of their own families.

She placed students into two groups and gave each group a book about farm workers to read and discuss. One group included all her Spanish speakers. She gave them a bilingual book, *César Chávez: The Struggle for Justice/César*

Chávez: La lucha por la justicia (del Castillo, 2002). She handed the other group a book in English, *Harvesting Hope: The Story of César Chávez* (Krull, 2003). After the groups read through their books and discussed them, the whole class discussed the competing interests and needs of farm workers and farm owners. As they engaged in this discussion, Ms. Tolland reminded them to draw on what they had read in their books.

Ms. Tolland also wanted to introduce concepts from the social studies standard that deals with agricultural and industrial development as it relates to the climate and the use of natural resources. She knew she could connect this concept to her students' lives since the farming city the school is in is growing, and new housing developments and shopping centers are replacing orchards and fields. The conflict between agriculture and industry has been featured on television and in the newspapers, so students are aware of the controversies surrounding this topic. In addition, a recent lack of rain in the area has led the city to impose water conservation measures.

Ms. Tolland organized the class into teams to research and debate these two issues. Over the next several days, students gathered information and met together to decide how to present their side of the controversy. The first two teams focused on the needs of farmers and those of developers. They realized that both groups were attempting to meet people's needs. The farmers produced the food citizens needed, and the developers built houses and shopping centers that were necessary as well.

The other two teams conducted research to find out where local water came from, how much water was allocated to the city, and how much water was used for agricultural purposes. Again, they recognized that people needed water in their homes but also needed food that the water helped produce. As Ms. Tolland's students studied and debated these issues, they became engaged in social studies because their studies connected so well to their lives. As they investigated these issues, the students developed important social studies concepts related to the state standards.

Ms. Tolland began this unit by asking her students to discuss and write about the contrasting pictures in *America: My Land, Your Land, Our Land*. This discussion and writing led naturally to consideration of issues in the community directly tied to the social studies standards. Ms. Tolland organized her class in a way that engaged her students by connecting social studies concepts to their lives. She moved away from a traditional method of teaching and connected the curriculum to her students' backgrounds. By using bilingual materials and putting students who spoke the same language together in a group, Ms. Tolland drew on her students' language strengths as well. Teachers, like Ms. Tolland, who use culturally relevant materials and build on their students' background knowledge, including their first languages, support their students' academic success. Ms. Tolland's attitude toward her students' languages and backgrounds was positive, and this helped form a classroom environment in which all students felt respected and valued.

We began with this scenario to set the stage for our discussion of language attitudes and bilingual education theory and research. We believe that teachers should understand the theory and know about the research that supports bilingual education even if they cannot provide bilingual education for their students. After reviewing this theory and research, we outline specific strategies that all teachers can implement to draw on their students' first languages and cultures. These include using culturally relevant texts, teaching cognates, and using the preview/view/review technique.

Attitudes Toward Students' Primary Languages

English language learners come to the United States from all over the world, and many large school districts across the country report as many as a hundred different home languages. Over the years, immigrants have encountered different attitudes toward their first languages. These attitudes have influenced their school success. Ruíz (1984) has described the historical development of three different orientations toward language: language-as-a-handicap, language-as-a-right, and language-as-a-resource. He defines an orientation as a "complex of dispositions toward language and its role, and toward languages and their role in society" (p. 16). Attitudes people hold about language come from their orientation.

During the 1950s and 60s, language-as-a-handicap was the prevalent orientation. Ruíz points out that at this time, educators saw ELLs as having a problem, even a handicap, so that "teaching English, even at the expense of the first language, became the objective of school programs" (p. 19). In other words, educators with this orientation believed that to overcome the handicap they had, ELLs must transition into English as quickly as possible.

Ruíz explains that in the 1970s, the language-as-a-right orientation emerged. As a part of the civil rights movement, bilingual educators called for the rights of non-native English speakers to bilingual education. Students in bilingual programs could exercise their right to maintain their native language while learning a second language. Those who held this orientation demanded freedom from discrimination on the basis of language and the right to use one's first language in daily living. While this language-as-a-right orientation is positive, Ruíz notes that many people were resentful, especially when language rights were enforced.

More recently, a third orientation, language-as-a-resource, has developed in some parts of the country. Ruíz sees this orientation as a better approach to language planning for several reasons:

> It can have a direct impact on enhancing the language status of subordinate languages; it can help to ease tensions between majority and minority communities; it can serve as a more consistent way of viewing the role of non-English languages in U.S. society; and it highlights the importance of cooperative language planning (pp. 25–26).

Currently, the best examples of the language-as-a-resource perspective are dual language programs. In these programs, ELLs' primary languages are developed as well as English, and native English speakers also learn a second language. Bilingualism is valued by all those involved in the programs.

At the same time that dual language programs are promoted in some communities, there is a widespread movement in the United States calling for English only. There seems to be a return to the language-as-a-handicap orientation as many educators blame the lack of academic success of several immigrant children on their inability to use English and their reliance on their first language. Certainly the passing of English-only legislation in California, Arizona, and Massachusetts reveals the lack of understanding of bilingual education and the theory and research that support it.

Theoretical Rationale and Research Support for Bilingual Education

Ser bilingüe es como vivir en dos mundos. Uno puede hablar con personas en español y entrar en su mundo. Lo mismo pasa cuando hablas, escribes y lees en inglés. Ahora que empecé el programa de educación bilingüe, puedo ver que tan valioso es ser bilingüe porque hay tantos niños que puedo ayudar en su primer idioma.

Translation

To be bilingual is like living in two worlds. One can speak to people in Spanish and enter into their world. The same thing happens when you speak, you write, and you read in English. Now that I have begun the bilingual education program, I can see how valuable it is to be bilingual because there are so many children that I can help in their first language.

This quote comes from Francisco, a college student who was just entering a teacher education program to become a bilingual teacher. Yvonne was his university advisor and instructor. Francisco came to the United States from El Salvador when he was 14. His mother, a migrant worker, had lived and worked for several years in the United States before she could bring Francisco and her other children to join her. She wanted a better life for them than was possible in their native country. By the time Francisco arrived in the United States, he was high-school age. Like most students who come at the secondary level, Francisco received no first language support. He was submersed in classes given only in English. His ESL classes focused on conversational language and did not prepare him for the academic demands of college.

Fortunately, Francisco was an outstanding soccer player. He attended a local Christian university on a soccer scholarship. He nearly dropped out of college because earning good grades was so difficult. Nevertheless, he persisted with encouragement from his mother and his coach. Because he struggled with English, he remained quiet in his college classes. When, as a senior, he did some observations in a first-grade bilingual classroom, Francisco saw for the first time how ELLs in a bilingual setting were able to participate fully in classroom activities. He noted that the children felt good about themselves as learners because they could draw on their first-language strengths as they studied school subjects. Francisco was inspired to use his bilingualism to help others so that they would not have to struggle as much as he had.

Cummins' Theories

Francisco had studied about bilingual theory, but it was when he saw the positive results in a classroom and compared those results to his English-only schooling that the theory became real to him. What theory can explain the consistently positive results of bilingual education? The key concept is Cummins' (2000) interdependence principle:

> To the extent that instruction in L_x is effective in promoting proficiency in L_x transfer of this proficiency to L_y will occur provided there is adequate exposure to L_y (either in school or the environment) and adequate motivation to learn L_y (p. 29).

In other words, when students are taught in and develop proficiency in their first language, L_x, that proficiency will transfer to the second language, L_y, assuming they are given enough exposure to the second language and are motivated to learn it. Cummins cites extensive research showing that there is a common proficiency that underlies specific languages. His *common underlying proficiency* (CUP) model holds that what we know in one language is accessible in a second language once we acquire sufficient proficiency in the second language.

To take a simple example, David learned about linguistics by studying in English. He knows about phonemes and syntax. David has also acquired a high intermediate level of Spanish. Even though he didn't study linguistics in Spanish, he can draw on his underlying knowledge of linguistics when speaking in Spanish. What he needs is knowledge of linguistics in English and enough of the grammar and vocabulary of Spanish to discuss linguistics in Spanish.

The concept of a common underlying proficiency helps explain why students like Stephanie, who enter school in the United States with grade-level skills in their first language, do so much better than students like Guillermo and Osman, who enter with limited formal schooling. Stephanie can transfer the knowledge and skills she developed in Spanish and apply them in studying subjects in English.

In addition, students who begin school speaking a language other than English do better in school when some of their instruction is in their native language. If all their instruction is in English, they won't understand the teacher and will fall behind. In contrast, as Krashen (1996) has pointed out, students in a bilingual class can learn academic content and develop the skills needed for problem solving and higher-order thinking in their first language while they become proficient in English.

When ELLs receive instruction in their first language for an extended period of time, they develop that language more fully. They then have the linguistic resources they need as they study English. Consider native English speakers who are taught entirely in English. They receive English language arts instruction throughout their schooling because two or three years would not be enough time for them to develop high levels of academic proficiency in English.

English language learners who live in an English-speaking environment do pick up English quickly, usually within one or two years. Many long-term English learners start school speaking a language other than English, but by the time they are in the second grade, most of them can understand and speak English quite well. However, the kind of English these students develop is what Cummins (1981) has termed *basic interpersonal communicative skills* (BICS), or conversational language. These students can follow directions, engage in games, and talk to their friends on the playground. However, many of them still struggle in school, and they fall further behind each year.

According to Cummins, these students have developed BICS, but they lack *cognitive academic language proficiency* (CALP), or academic language. Research has shown that the development of academic language takes from four to nine years (Collier, 1989). In Chapter 6 we elaborate on academic language further, explaining what it is and suggesting ways teachers can help students develop it. Students who are put into an all-English program or exited to an all-English program after only two or three years have not developed academic proficiency in their first language to transfer into English, and they are behind their native English-speaking classmates in their development of academic English. For that reason, they fall behind academically.

In contrast, students who receive primary language instruction for at least six years develop academic proficiency in their first language and subject-matter knowledge that they can draw on as they study in English. In good bilingual programs, students study part of the day in English and part of the day in their first language. If teachers teach language through content and organize around themes as they instruct in the two languages, ELLs develop both language proficiency and academic content knowledge.

A closer look at Francisco's educational experiences helps illustrate the effects an English-only program can have on students. When Francisco came to the United States as a freshman in high school, he was suddenly thrust into an all-English environment. Although he came to school reading and writing at grade level in Spanish, no advanced Spanish classes were offered at the high school. The school did offer ESL classes, so he began to develop English proficiency. However, these classes focused on conversational English rather than academic English. Francisco's academic development was delayed because none of the academic content subjects he needed were offered in Spanish. He could not continue his study of math or science while learning English. Instead, he was placed in ESL classes and non-college preparatory classes, such as physical education and shop. In fact, were it not for a soccer scholarship, he would not have continued his education beyond high school.

Even though Francisco's high school experiences delayed his academic and cognitive development and failed to provide academic language development in English or Spanish, Francisco succeeded in college due to his early interest in schooling and reading, his own perseverance, and the strong support of his mother, his soccer coach, and his native English-speaking girlfriend, whom he later married. However, many ELLs do not succeed academically. Research shows that programs with some first-language support show better academic results for students than English-only programs.

Research Support for Bilingual Education

Research studies that provide support for bilingual education generally compare the academic achievement in English as measured by standardized test scores of similar students in different types of programs. The assumption is that if the students enter school with similar backgrounds, then differences in test scores can be attributed to the model of instruction they receive. Since it takes from four to nine years to develop academic competence in a second language (Collier, 1989; Cummins, 1994), test scores for ELLs must be measured over time. For that reason, studies should be longitudinal.

An important early study was conducted by Ramírez (1991), who compared groups of students in three kinds of programs: structured English immersion, *early exit bilingual*, and *late exit bilingual*. The structured English immersion programs provided ESL support for English language learners but no primary language support or development. The early exit programs included teaching in the primary language until about second grade. Then instruction shifted entirely into English. Students in the late exit programs continued to receive primary language instruction through at least fourth grade. Ramírez concluded that students in the late exit programs had higher academic achievement than students in either of the other two programs. In addition, Ramírez noted that teaching students in their native language did not interfere with their acquisition of English.

Additional research support for bilingual education comes from the meta-analysis conducted by Greene (1998). In a meta-analysis, the researcher summarizes the results of a number of studies to draw general conclusions across the research. Greene examined 75 studies of bilingual programs. He chose 11 studies that met the minimal standards for the quality of their research design. He combined the statistical results of these studies, which included test score results of 2,719 students. Of these, 1,562 were enrolled in bilingual programs in 13 different states. Based on the results, Greene concluded that ELLs who are taught using at least some of their native language perform significantly better on standardized tests in English than similar children taught only in English. Thus, this meta-analysis reached the same conclusion as the large-scale, long-term study conducted by Ramírez.

Reviews of the research on bilingual education consistently show bilingual education is the best model for educating ELLs. A recent meta-analysis (Rolstad et al., 2005) incorporated many studies not covered in other reports and included more current research. Once again, the results favored bilingual education. The authors state:

> In the current study, we present a meta-analysis of studies comparing effects of instructional programs for ELL students in an effort to clarify "the big picture" in this debate. Our approach differs from previously conducted literature reviews in that it includes many studies not reviewed previously, and we did not exclude studies *a priori* based on design quality. Although our corpus and methodological approach differ from those of previous researchers, our conclusions are consistent with most of the major reviews conducted to date. We find an advantage for approaches that provide instruction in the students' first language and conclude that state and federal policies restricting or discouraging the use of the native language in programs for ELL students cannot be justified by a reasonable consideration of the evidence (p. 574).

The researchers found that bilingual education was more beneficial for ELLs than all-English approaches. They also found that students in developmental bilingual programs, such as dual language programs, outperformed those in short-term programs. In general, the longer students received primary language instruction, the better they did on academic measures of English.

The studies discussed here involved large numbers of students over long periods of time. The researchers concluded that the use of the native language for instruction resulted in increased academic achievement for ELLs. However, native language instructional support is often not an option in schools. In the remainder of this chapter, we will address ways that teachers can effectively support their ELLs by drawing on their first languages and cultures even when the teachers do not speak the students' languages.

Preview/View/Review

One excellent strategy for working with ELLs is *preview/view/review* (Y. Freeman & D. Freeman, 2002; Y. Freeman & D. Freeman, 1998). This strategy can work in classes with ELLs from one or several primary language backgrounds, and it can work whether or not the teacher speaks the students' languages. An example might come from a teacher who has organized around the theme "How does the weather affect our lives?" This lesson is designed to teach students about different kinds of clouds.

The teacher asks a bilingual student, a bilingual cross-age tutor, a bilingual paraprofessional, or a parent to briefly tell the ELLs in their native language that this will be a lesson about five kinds of clouds. This brief introduction provides the ELLs with a preview of the lesson. Other ways to provide a preview include having a bilingual student, paraprofessional, or parent read a book about clouds in the students' primary language. In addition, a teacher could show a video clip about clouds with narration in the students' first language. A teacher could also have students brainstorm in same-language groups what they already know about clouds. Students could use their first languages in their groups and then report back in English.

During the view part, the teacher conducts a lesson using strategies to make the input comprehensible. The teacher shows pictures of different kinds of clouds and writes the names of the cloud formations and their characteristics under the pictures. With the help of the preview, the students can follow the English better and acquire both English and academic content.

Finally, it is good to have a short time of review during which students can use their native language. For example, students who speak the same first language could meet again in groups to review the main ideas of the lesson, ask questions, and clarify their understanding, and then report back in English. Figure 4.1 outlines the preview/view/review technique.

The preview/view/review technique provides a structured way to alternate English and native-language instruction. Students are given access to the academic concepts they need to know and, at the same time, acquire English. Simply translating everything into a student's first language is not productive because the student will tune out English, the language that is harder to understand. This *concurrent translation method* does not lead to either concept or language acquisition. Using preview/view/ review can help teachers avoid concurrent translation while still drawing on students' first languages.

Figure 4.1: **Preview/View/Review**

> ### Preview
> #### first language
> Students are given an overview of the lesson or activity in their first language. (This could be an oral summary, a short reading, a film, a key question, etc.)
>
> ### View
> #### second or target language [English]
> The teacher teaches the lesson or directs the activity in the students' second language.
>
> ### Review
> #### first language
> Students summarize key ideas and raise questions about the lesson in their first language and report back in English.

Accessing Cognates

Earlier in this chapter we discussed Cummins' interdependence principle, which holds that what we know in one language is accessible in a second language. Cummins further points out that to the extent languages are related, specific features will transfer. Spanish and English are closely related languages, and teachers can draw on Spanish speakers' vocabulary in their first language to build the academic language they need in

English. There are many cognates in languages like Spanish and English. Cognates are literally words that are "born together" or come from the same root. The words may be pronounced or spelled differently, but they are generally recognizable across languages. For example, the English word *alphabet* and the Spanish word *alfabeto* are cognates.

Although English is a Germanic language, many of the scholarly terms in the English vocabulary have Latin and Greek roots. According to Corson (1995), about 60 percent of the English words used in texts come from Greek and Latin sources. Since Spanish derives from Latin, many common words in Spanish are academic words in English. One point that Cummins makes is that transfer of knowledge and skills, such as the knowledge of cognates, does not occur automatically. Teachers need to facilitate the process with specific lessons. Teachers can help Spanish speakers develop academic language by making connections between the everyday Spanish terms and English academic vocabulary.

Williams (2001) suggests that teachers photocopy a page from a textbook, project it on an overhead transparency, and work with students to identify words that are cognates. Following this whole-class activity, students can work in pairs to find cognates on photocopied pages of their texts. Williams also suggests that teachers can create a classroom cognate wall or dictionary. Students can add to the list throughout the year.

Rodríguez (2001) also advocates using cognates to teach Spanish speakers. He suggests specific strategy lessons designed to increase students' awareness of cognates. For example, after reading a short passage and discussing the content, students can work in pairs to identify cognates. They can be given a second version of the text in which the cognates are replaced by words with Germanic roots. Students can determine the meanings of the new words by comparing them with the cognates. What is important in lessons like this is to focus students' attention specifically on cognates to help them understand academic texts in English.

Rodríguez provides a helpful list of the types of cognates that teachers might present. He notes that while some words retain the same spelling (*hotel*), others show a predictable variation. For example, *–tion* in English becomes *–ción* in Spanish *(declaration, declaración)*. Some cognates are less apparent but share the same root *(sport, deporte)*. Some sound alike even though the spellings vary *(pleasure, placer)*. Some words are cognates for one meaning but not for another. In English, the word *letter* has two meanings, but in Spanish it has only one. *Letra* refers to a character of the alphabet. A good exercise would be for students to collect cognates and sort them into these categories.

The articles by Rodríguez and Williams include helpful ideas for teaching students about Spanish-English cognates. English also has cognates with many other languages, and a study of these related languages can be fascinating to students. While we were living for a short period in Lithuania, we noticed that the ingredients on the back of the cornflakes package were given in 13 languages. A look at the words for those ingredients sparked a fascinating discussion. For example, *corn* in German is *mais*, much like *maíz* in Spanish. But in Slovenian, it is *koruza*, perhaps closer to English. In Lithuanian, Latvian, Polish, Czech, Serbo-Croatian, Slovakian, and Hungarian, the words for *corn* all begin with *kukur-* and have different endings. Discussions about these cognates help students and teachers become more aware of word roots, spellings, and meanings.

Using preview/view/review and accessing cognates are just two ways teachers can draw on students' first-language strengths even when the teachers don't speak those languages. In the following section, we provide other simple ways teachers can validate and promote the use of students' primary languages.

Ten Tips for Supporting Students' First Languages

Once teachers understand the theory and research base for bilingual education, they often try to think of ways to help their students draw on their first languages even if the teachers are not bilingual themselves. We have taken the successful strategies used by teachers we have worked with and have developed a list of ways teachers can support their students' first languages (D. Freeman & Y. Freeman, 1993, 2001; Y. Freeman & D. Freeman, 1991). Figure 4.2 lists these tips.

Figure 4.2: **Ten Tips for Supporting Students' Primary Languages**

> **1.** Arrange for books to be read to students in their primary languages.
>
> **2.** Organize bilingual tutoring.
>
> **3.** Organize pen-pal letter writing.
>
> **4.** Pair newcomers with a partner who speaks the same primary language.
>
> **5.** Use primary-language storytellers.
>
> **6.** Build a classroom library in students' primary languages.
>
> **7.** Encourage primary-language journal writing.
>
> **8.** Publish books written in students' primary languages.
>
> **9.** Ensure that classroom environmental print represents students' primary languages.
>
> **10.** Allow ELLs to talk in their primary languages.

Tip #1: Arrange for books to be read to students in their primary languages.

Teachers can arrange for bilingual paraprofessionals or parent volunteers to read to the students in their primary language. Georgiana, a first-grade teacher who had both Spanish-speaking students and students who spoke Southeast Asian languages, did this regularly. She set up a schedule at the beginning of the year for bilingual parents to come into the classroom and read. Sometimes the parents had their own books in the first language, but at other times she drew from her own collection of books in Spanish, Hmong, Vietnamese, Khmer, and Laotian. (See Tip #6 for ideas about how to find bilingual books in different languages.) She invited parents to come in before it was their turn, to watch her read to the children. Those parents who followed up on this suggestion read with more expression and showed pictures more often than parents who never watched her demonstrations. Georgiana also found that parents were often shy about reading, but if she gave them the books ahead of time to practice, they were much more confident. Georgiana noticed how proud the children were when their parents came to class to read. All the children were interested in hearing books read in other languages, even when they did not speak the languages.

Tip #2: Organize bilingual tutoring.

A second way to support students' first languages is for teachers to invite older students who speak the first languages of the children in a lower grade to come on a regular basis to read to or with the younger students and to provide previews and reviews in their primary languages (Samway et al., 1995). For example, sixth-grade students might come to a first-grade class two or three mornings a week to read to a younger student who speaks the same language. In addition, younger students can choose books to read in their first languages to the older students on certain days. This often proves beneficial to the older students because they see that their first-language skills are useful and important.

Susana, a second-grade teacher, was concerned that her Vietnamese students were not getting enough first-language support in Vietnamese. The one Vietnamese paraprofessional in the school came into her classroom for a half hour twice a week, but she kept trying to teach English to the children instead of reinforcing key concepts in Vietnamese as Susana suggested. When a fifth-grade teacher commented on how he was struggling to motivate some of his fifth-grade Vietnamese students, Susana had an idea. Working with the fifth-grade teacher, she arranged for those students to come into her classroom at a regular time each day, when they were not missing important content instruction, to become tutors. Susana worked with these students several days after school, explaining how she wanted them to be "Vietnamese teachers" for her students. She and the students reviewed the second-grade science content standard about how living things interact with each other. She showed the students the science books in English that her students were reading, and she and the fifth graders talked about how living organisms adapt to their environment to survive. They read about the emperor penguins that live on Snow Hill Island in the Antarctic and about boa constrictors whose favorite habitat is the rain forest.

Susana asked the fifth graders to use these books and summarize in Vietnamese some key characteristics of the animals and the habitats they lived in. The next day when the fifth graders arrived and began working with the Vietnamese students, the fifth graders first summarized the books for the younger students in Vietnamese. Then they helped the younger students draw pictures of the animals and their habitats and make lists of the characteristics of the animals that allowed them to adapt to their environments. The half-hour science period went by quickly for Susana's Vietnamese students because they were so engaged in the lesson. Later, the fifth-grade teacher came to Susana and told her how excited his students had been when they returned from her classroom. He asked if they could continue this tutoring because he believed it was just what his students needed to raise their self-esteem and encourage them to work harder.

Tip #3: Organize pen-pal letter writing.

A third way to help students maintain and develop their primary languages is to encourage them to write using their first language. An authentic way to do this is to have them write letters to someone else who speaks that language. Yvonne asked her bilingual student teachers to write in Spanish to children in Sam's first-grade bilingual class. Her original intent was to have the student teachers analyze the children's spelling development in Spanish. However, the activity proved to have many other benefits. Sam's first graders looked forward to the letters and increased their vocabulary by reading the letters. The children also were encouraged to write more as they had a lot to tell their pen pals. At the end of the semester, the first graders came to the university campus for a visit to a college classroom where the student teachers read to them in Spanish and treated them to a special lunch.

Other teachers have organized pen-pal letters between students in different classes in their school. They have their students write to their pen pals in their first language. Some teachers have been able to find teachers in other countries whose students can be pen pals. For example, a teacher in the United States might have her Spanish speakers write to students in a class in Mexico. The students can learn about similarities and differences between their schools and their communities. As teachers everywhere have greater access to the Internet, it has become easier to arrange for their ELLs to e-mail students in other countries who speak their first language.

Tip #4: Pair newcomers with a partner who speaks the same primary language.

When newcomers enter a mainstream classroom where the teacher does not speak their first language, they are often overwhelmed by the new setting, different expectations, and the new language. An excellent way to support these newcomers is to assign them a first-language buddy. This buddy system is particularly helpful for introducing new students to class routines.

Buddies should give newcomers a tour of the school, accompany them to lunch, and orient them to classes like physical education. Within the classroom, buddies can provide a preview and review in the newcomer's primary language.

It is important to make the position of being a buddy one of prestige. Teachers should make it clear to students that they were chosen to be buddies because of their special bilingual abilities. Teachers who give the buddies some guidelines and spend time helping buddies understand how to help the newcomers have more success than those who simply pair students.

Rhoda, a fifth-grade teacher in a rural California school, assigned Felipe to be the buddy of a newcomer, Juan, who had just arrived from Guadalajara. At first, Felipe didn't want to be with the new student who couldn't speak English, but Rhoda explained to him how important it was to be chosen for this position. When Felipe began to provide previews for Juan in Spanish, Juan responded enthusiastically and appreciatively. Soon the two boys became fast friends and spent time together outside of class. Both boys had a passion for soccer. An added benefit was that Felipe's Spanish vocabulary began to grow. As Felipe provided previews and reviews in Spanish for Juan, Juan would sometimes summarize to be sure he understood, using words that Felipe didn't know in Spanish. The two boys were often seen with the Spanish/English dictionary looking up Spanish words and discussing them. Rhoda knew that her buddy pairing was beneficial for both boys when Felipe told her one day, "Teacher, I'm helping Juan, but he's teaching me more Spanish!"

Tip #5: Use primary-language storytellers.

Often, newcomers come from cultures with a tradition of storytelling. In fact, storytelling is often the way elders teach children to reason, to live a moral life, and to value cultural traditions. All good storytellers use gestures and other devices to make their stories comprehensible. Sometimes the stories are universal, ones that English-speaking teachers and children know. Well-known stories such as "Cinderella" and "Three Billy Goats Gruff" have counterparts (and origins) in non-English languages. One successful activity that has benefits for all the students is to invite bilingual storytellers to come to the class and tell familiar stories.

Katie, a kindergarten teacher, had many ELLs in her class. She had found books in Spanish, and her bilingual paraprofessional frequently read and discussed these books with her Spanish-speakers. However, Katie also had several Hmong children who spoke little English and were often reluctant to participate in class. Katie learned that a Hmong storyteller was available to come to classes to tell stories in Hmong, so she invited him to come to her class to tell "Three Billy Goats Gruff." Before the storyteller arrived, Katie read several versions of the folktale to her class in English. They also acted out the story with children taking the parts of the troll and the three goats. The day the storyteller arrived, ready to take the Hmong students off to a corner to tell his tale, Katie asked him to tell the story to the entire class in Hmong. She reasoned that the children knew the story so well that they would be able to follow along. She was right. When the storyteller told the part of the story where the goats cross the bridge, the students shouted in delight at the "Trip trap, trip trap" spoken in Hmong. All the children, no matter what their language background, enjoyed the story.

The storytelling in Hmong was a positive experience for all Katie's students, but her support for her Hmong students' primary language paid added dividends. In the days that followed the storytelling, Mo, a quiet Hmong boy, proved that he could not only learn but also teach. First, Mo wrote and drew in his journal about his favorite story, "Three Billy Goats Gruff." Then Mo became a "teacher" of Hmong to his own teacher. Mo drew pictures of clothing and school items and labeled them using invented spellings in Hmong. Below the pictures, he wrote in English, "theys are mog log wich theys are the thine to me" ("These are Hmong language. These are the thing to me.") Katie responded by telling him how much she liked reading his Hmong. Katie reported that from the time of the visit from the Hmong storyteller, Mo showed not only a pride in his first language and culture but also an enthusiasm for school not evident before.

Tip #6: Build a classroom library in students' primary languages.

When they are available, bilingual books representing the different languages in their classrooms can be used by teachers. Some publishers have dedicated themselves to finding bilingual books for teachers, and online searches can help teachers locate books they need. For example, at the International Children's Digital Library (http://www.icdlbooks.org), children can choose to read books in English or other languages including Arabic, simplified Chinese, and Tagalog (Filipino). At http://www.panap.com, teachers can locate bilingual books for children in 35 languages ranging from Arabic to Yoruba. At http://www.shens.com, there are multicultural books from Asian countries and Latin America. For some time, Cinco Puntos Press (http://www.cincopuntos.com) has produced engaging bilingual books in Spanish and English.

Teachers can use these bilingual books for oral and written language development in English by asking students to talk about and write about the books in English. Students can use these books to develop their first language, or they can use the first-language text as a resource when they are reading in English. In addition, teachers and students can carry out language comparisons by looking together at texts in English and another language.

When money is not available to purchase bilingual books, teachers and administrators must get creative. One principal wanted to provide books in different languages in every classroom for his multilingual student body. He bought one copy each of more than 200 books that were bilingual or written in languages other than English. Then he bought ten book carts for the school. He worked with the teachers to organize the new books on the carts. Each teacher could take a cart and keep it for several weeks. Then the carts were rotated to another classroom. When educators provide books in ELLs' primary languages, they demonstrate that their students' first languages are valued and, by extension, that their students are also valued.

Tip #7: Encourage primary-language journal writing.

Allowing students to write in their journals in their first language is especially important for newcomers. Otherwise, students who do not speak or understand much English do not use journal-writing time effectively. They may be able to copy a few words in English, but the activity does not allow them to write about themselves in personal journals, respond to content learning in content journals, or react to reading in their literature journals. Often, students understand more of what is happening in English than they can show in English. When students are allowed to respond in their primary language to what they have understood of the English language instruction, they deepen their comprehension and also begin to transfer complex ideas and vocabulary to English.

Elena could speak Spanish and provide previews and reviews for her newcomer Spanish speakers. However, when a new Korean girl, Kim, came to her classroom and could not communicate in English, Elena felt lost. Elena teaches around content themes, uses lots of comprehensible reading, including big books, and engages her students in hands-on activities. Kim watched what Elena and the other students were doing but remained silent for the first few weeks. Elena was frustrated that she was getting no response from Kim and wondered if she was learning anything.

One day when Kim was sitting quietly while the other students were writing in journals about what they had done in class that day, Elena decided to try asking Kim to write too. She gave Kim a journal and, with gestures, helped her to understand that she could write about the class activities in Korean. At first, Kim didn't want to write in Korean, but with encouragement she tried. Soon Kim was writing quite a lot, but Elena could not tell what she was writing. When Kim's mother came to pick her up that day, Elena asked her to read Kim's journal. Kim's mother explained that the writing wasn't always conventional, but she was writing about insects that the class had studied in science and about a story the class had read about a little boy and a butterfly.

Over the next weeks, Elena encouraged Kim to continue writing in the journal. Several times Kim showed her journal to Elena and by pointing to books and things around the room, was able to "tell" Elena what she was writing. After six weeks, Kim began to write some words and even write partial sentences in English. The important lesson that Elena learned was that Kim was able to use her primary language to show what she was learning while she was acquiring the English she needed to begin to communicate in English.

Tip #8: Publish books written in students' primary languages.

Even when teachers are able to purchase some books in their students' primary languages for their classroom libraries, there are never enough. To increase the primary-language resources in classrooms, schools or districts can rely on resource teachers to create books, and teachers can publish books of student writing. These are good strategies to use when few commercially published books are available in a language.

One example comes from Doua Vu, the only Hmong bilingual resource teacher for a large school district. She wanted Hmong children in the district to learn Hmong and, at the same time, appreciate their cultural heritage, something she saw slipping away as children became assimilated into the English-dominant culture. Doua took pictures of children dressing up in traditional clothing to celebrate the Hmong New Year. Then she used those pictures to write a predictable bilingual book, *Dressing Up to Go to Hmong New Year/Hnav Tsoos Hmoob Mus Tom Tshav Pob*, that she photocopied in color. Teachers throughout the district used her book with their children, thus validating the children's first language, Hmong, and also celebrating the importance of the Hmong New Year.

Teresa, a second-grade teacher, also found a way to support primary-language book publishing. After a class discussion on the importance of being bilingual, Navy, a Cambodian student, pointed out that there were no books in the classroom in her native language, Khmer. When Teresa invited her to write one, Navy took recess and lunchtime for several days to produce a book of letters, numbers, and words that would teach her classmates and the teacher Khmer. Teresa had the book laminated and put in the class library, where it became a favorite. Other students sought out Navy to explain the Khmer alphabet and to teach them how to say the letters, numbers, and words. Classroom publishing of books in other languages provides a positive experience for all the students in the classroom.

Tip #9: Ensure that classroom environmental print represents students' primary languages.

It is important that the environmental print in classrooms and in the school halls represents the languages of the children in the school. One high school teacher had students make bookmarks that were laminated and left in a basket for visitors. On one side of these beautifully decorated bookmarks was a proverb in English, and on the other, the equivalent proverb written in the languages of her students: Chinese, Spanish, Hmong, Russian, Khmer, and Vietnamese. Visitors were fascinated with these bookmarks and quizzed students on the various alphabets that they used.

Betty, a kindergarten teacher, had students whose first languages were Vietnamese, Russian, Khmer, and Hmong. Betty sought the help of bilingual paraprofessionals and parents to put the color words up around the room in the different languages of her students. Although her kindergartners were just beginning to learn how to read and write, she found the children constantly looking at the words written in different scripts. One Cambodian girl walked up to Betty one day and pulled on her skirt to get her attention. "Teacher," she said, pointing to the word *orange* written in Khmer, "that's me." This touching incident shows how much the inclusion of their languages means to children.

Several schools we have visited that have English- and Spanish-speaking children have welcome signs in Spanish and English, labels in both languages, and books in the library and in the hall in both languages. In addition, students' work in both languages is hung up in the halls, showing that both languages are equally valued.

Tip #10: Allow ELLs to talk in their primary languages.

Sometimes teachers believe that prohibiting students from speaking in their first language will keep them from depending on their first language and encourage them to use more English. However, just the opposite is true. Students need to express themselves. When they cannot speak English, they often become silent and disengaged from what is happening in the classroom. When they tune out, they are not learning either content or English. It is essential to keep students engaged. Allowing them to use their first language is one way to do this.

When students are working on a project, teachers can sometimes group together students who speak the same first language. The students can use their first language to clarify concepts for each other as they complete their tasks in English. Another strategy is to have students turn and talk in their primary language at specific times to summarize key ideas taught in English.

Teachers can allow younger students to use their primary language during share time. Bilingual students or paraprofessionals can translate the key ideas. This benefits the non-English speakers because they have to organize their thoughts and explain their ideas orally. It also benefits all the students to hear another language and to see their peers, who may be silent during much of the day when instruction is in English, speak with confidence.

A good example of the importance of allowing students to use their first language in class comes from a visit Yvonne and David made to a school in Iowa. The school had experienced a recent influx of Spanish speakers whose parents had found work with local meat-packing companies. The administration wanted Yvonne to demonstrate to teachers how a bilingual lesson might look. Yvonne began the lesson with a group of first graders that included both native English and native Spanish speakers. Most of the Spanish speakers were somewhat bilingual, except for Javier, who spoke almost no English.

First Yvonne provided a preview for the native English speakers. She explained in English that she was going to read a big book in Spanish, but that it would be understandable to the students because the pictures told the story quite well. Then Yvonne showed the book and asked the students in Spanish what they thought the book might be about. Javier's hand shot up, and he participated enthusiastically every time Yvonne used Spanish in her extended lesson. In fact, at one point Yvonne had to ask Javier to give some of the other students a chance to talk too.

At the end of the demonstration, Javier's teacher came up to Yvonne in tears. She realized that Javier was a very competent student when instruction was given in his first language. She admitted to Yvonne, "I thought he might have serious learning problems." Seeing Javier as an enthusiastic participant helped his teacher and Javier's peers see him in a completely new light. This experience also gave Javier increased confidence in his ability to do well in school in a new country and a new language.

The ten tips we provide here are only a beginning. Creative teachers constantly come up with ways they can support their students' first languages and cultures. Once teachers see how the use of the first language encourages learners and promotes learning in English, they are convinced that the efforts they have made are worthwhile. We end this chapter by discussing one other way that teachers can draw on students' primary languages and cultural backgrounds: by using culturally relevant books.

Culturally Relevant Books

Krashen (2004) points out that the more people read, the more their reading comprehension will improve and the more capable they will be of reading from a variety of genres, including academic content texts. For bilingual children, the best approach is to develop their first-language literacy and ensure they have many opportunities to read in both their first and second languages. When ELLs are being instructed in English, they need the additional support that comes through engagement with texts that connect to their cultural backgrounds.

Research shows that students read better and read more when they read culturally relevant books (Y. Freeman et al., 2003; Goodman, 1982; R. Jiménez, 1997). Developing a collection of culturally relevant texts takes a concerted effort. Not all books about Spanish speakers, for example, are relevant to all Hispanic students. Some books merely perpetuate stereotypes. Others, especially those published in Spain, contain settings and events that are unfamiliar to most Latino students in the United States. Still other books contain fairy tales or legends, and students have trouble connecting personally to such books. However, an increasing number of culturally relevant books are being published.

Just what makes a book culturally relevant? Figure 4.3 provides a rubric that teachers and students can use to determine whether or not a book is culturally relevant.

Teachers we have worked with have used the rubric in various ways. Some have read a book that they thought might be culturally relevant to a single ELL and then asked the questions on the rubric. They have been excited about how the children connect to the events and can extend the reading by comparing characters and events to their own families and experiences. Other teachers have had older students read a book they believed fit the questions on the rubric and then had students individually fill out the rubric. Still others have used the rubric as a basis for class discussion of a text they read aloud to the class or that the class read for a literature study. In the following section, we give examples of books that fit each question from the rubric.

Figure 4.3: **Cultural Relevance Rubric**

1. Are the characters in the story like you and your family?

Just like us			Not at all
4	3	2	1

2. Have you ever had an experience like one described in this story?

Yes			No
4	3	2	1

3. Have you lived in or visited places like those in the story?

Yes			No
4	3	2	1

4. Could this story take place this year?

Yes			No
4	3	2	1

5. How close do you think the main characters are to you in age?

Very close			Not close at all
4	3	2	1

6. Are there main characters in the story who are boys (for boys) or girls (for girls)?

Yes			No
4	3	2	1

7. Do the characters talk like you and your family do?

Yes			No
4	3	2	1

8. How often do you read stories like these?

Often			Never
4	3	2	1

Question #1: Are the characters in the story like you and your family?

Francisco is a third-grade bilingual teacher working with Hispanic children in a small city on the California coast. He recently received Ada's *I Love Saturdays y domingos* (2002) as a gift because he and his Anglo wife have a 4-year-old daughter. The characters in this book mirror his own family. The book is about a girl who spends Saturdays with her English-speaking Anglo grandparents and Sundays (*domingos*) with her Spanish-speaking Hispanic grandparents.

Francisco read the story to his class and then explained that his daughter, Maya Esmeralda, has English-speaking and Spanish-speaking grandparents like the characters in the story. This led to a discussion of what the children in the class did with their grandparents, whether they spoke English or Spanish with them, and lots of questions for the teacher about his new daughter, what languages he and his wife spoke with her, and how important it was to be bilingual.

Jennifer, a kindergarten teacher in the inner city, has ELLs from all over the world in her classroom. She recently found a multicultural limited-text big book that is relevant to her students, *Rice All Day* (Tsang, 2003). Her students were fascinated as they read about Lin from China, who has rice for breakfast; Luis from Mexico, who has *horchata*, a Mexican rice drink, at lunch; and Waleed, who has a Middle Eastern rice-and-lentils dish for dinner.

Question #2: Have you ever had an experience like one described in this story?

When Sandra read *La tortillería* and the English version, *The Tortilla Factory* (Paulsen, 1995a, 1995b) to her newcomers from rural Mexico who had had limited formal schooling, she discovered that culturally relevant texts can lead to content learning, reading, and writing. This book describes how corn seeds are planted, grown, harvested, and made into tortillas that nourish the workers, who then plant more corn. As Sandra read the book, her indigenous students from Oaxaca, Mexico, kept interrupting her to tell her they had planted corn, harvested it, and ground it into flour and made tortillas by hand, as shown in the pictures in the book.

The class decided that the students from Oaxaca should demonstrate all the steps involved in turning corn into tortillas. After the class had discussed the process and the materials needed for the activity, Sandra bought the ingredients, and the students brought the necessary utensils from home. Her indigenous Triqui and Mixteco students, who usually acted ashamed of their culture and language, became the experts. These students demonstrated the steps while the other students took notes on the whole process.

Sandra used this culturally relevant book as part of her unit on plants and seeds. The reading and demonstration helped her students understand the steps involved in the cycle of planting seeds, harvesting them, and then turning them into food that gives workers strength to plant more seeds. All her students were engaged, and they developed both literacy skills and content knowledge through the activities Sandra developed around this book.

Another book that relates to many ELLs' experiences is *Friends From the Other Side/Amigos del otro lado* (Anzaldúa, 1993). This book is especially appropriate for third through fifth graders who live along the border of the United States and Mexico. When teachers in South Texas read this book about a young girl who helps a young boy and his mother from "the other side," discussion frequently turns to illegals, an often-ignored reality along the border. Students who were born in the United States study alongside others who either cross the border daily or who live in fear of deportation until they can arrange legal papers. Discussion of the events in this story helps students think about the dynamics in their own classroom community. The book brings to the surface the human elements of suffering and alienation and encourages students to talk about their prejudices and fears.

Nancy has many refugee children in her urban third-grade classroom. These children suffer from different kinds of trauma and often need to share their experiences in a positive way. She reads *Marianthe's Story: Painted Words and Spoken Memories* (Aliki, 1998) to them. This is a two-part book about a refugee girl from Greece. In the first part of the book, the girl is a kindergartner who does not yet speak English but is able to draw pictures to represent some of her traumatic experiences. The second part of the picture book, which is read by turning the book over and starting at the back, is about this same girl in elementary school who can now write in her journal and share her story in English. Nancy's students are not from Greece, but many of them have had experiences like those of the main character in this story.

Question #3: Have you lived in or visited places like those in the story?

Oscar, a high school developmental reading teacher in a rural community, works with long-term English learners. Many of his students' parents are migrant workers. Two books that are culturally relevant for these students are *The Circuit* (F. Jiménez, 1997) and *Breaking Through* (F. Jiménez, 2001). The first book describes the elementary school years of a migrant child, and the second book follows this student's progress through high school. The author writes about the area Oscar's students live in, talks about places his students know, and describes experiences that are like those that the students or their relatives have had. The students are interested in these books, and they eagerly discuss the events in the stories.

Another book that is appropriate for urban middle and junior high school ELLs from different cultures is *One City, One School, Many Foods* (Palacios, 1997). The book describes students from different countries who now live in New York City. It shows them eating at home with their families and describes meals from the Dominican Republic, Korea, Africa, Uzbekistan, and China. This book provides many opportunities for discussion of cultural differences. Students can compare and contrast foods from different countries.

Question #4: Could this story take place this year?

When Yvonne read *Going Home* (Bunting, 1998) to her graduate class, she quickly realized that this book was especially relevant for teachers. In this story, two children raised in the United States reluctantly travel back to rural Mexico with their parents to spend Christmas with relatives there. On the trip, they begin to understand the sacrifices their parents have made for them. After reading the story, one teary-eyed teacher raised her hand and said, "That story taught me how important it is that my students go back to Mexico for the holidays. I've always complained and wondered why parents take their children out of school. I understand a bit better now."

The following week, a high school teacher reported that she had read the book to her students and that the reading had led to a discussion that caused several of her students to talk about how their views of living in the United States were different from their parents' views and how hard it was for them and their parents to understand and appreciate each other. The book is especially valuable because it reflects the current reality of many Mexican-American students.

The Name Jar (Choi, 2001) is another book that deals with current realities. In this story, a Korean girl goes to school in the United States for the first time. On the bus to school, someone asks her what her name is, and all the children laugh at how it sounds. Once she gets to her classroom, she refuses to tell anyone her name. After several days, the teacher devises a way to give the girl a name by putting out a jar and asking the children to write a name for her and put it in the jar. At the end, the children discover her real name and its beautiful meaning, and everyone puts her real name in the jar.

Question #5: How close do you think the main characters are to you in age?

Barbara teaches in a rural school where many of the students are from migrant families. She finds that her native Spanish-speaking first graders love to hear her read stories that relate to their experiences and are also about children their own age. One story her students enjoy is *La mariposa* (F. Jiménez, 1998). This book was originally a chapter of *The Circuit* (F. Jiménez, 1997) and is now a children's book beautifully illustrated by Simon Silva. Barbara reads the Spanish version of the book first, and the students discuss it. Her students tell her, *"Es triste porque Francisco no tiene amigos"* (It's sad because Francisco doesn't have friends), and they connect to his brother Roberto helping him. They tell her, *"Mi hermano me lleva a la escuela también, maestra"* (My brother takes me to school too, teacher).

Later in the year, while the students are engaged in an insect unit, she reminds them of the story she had read earlier in Spanish. That reading serves as a preview as she now reads them the English version. In the story, the young boy sits in the back of the class and observes a caterpillar that turns into a butterfly. The metamorphosis parallels the change the young boy is going through. Barbara's students relate this part of the story to the cocoon they have been watching in their own classroom as part of their insect unit.

Question #6: Are there main characters in the story who are boys (for boys) or girls (for girls)?

Linda teaches ESL in an urban high school. One book she reads to her students is *América Is Her Name* (Rodríguez, 1997). This book is about a girl from Oaxaca, Mexico, whose family moves to a large city in the United States. Linda's female students find this book especially relevant because the character, América, is a high school girl who struggles with teachers and family members who don't understand her. América develops pride in her cultural roots. Although her ESL teacher speaks only English, a visiting poet who speaks Spanish comes to América's class. He encourages the students to recite poetry. América stands and recites a poem she learned in Mexico. Later, she writes a poem that wins a citywide contest. The girls in Linda's class enjoy reading about América, an immigrant girl who overcomes obstacles to succeed in the new country.

Linda has also found books that the boys in her class connect to. One book almost all the boys enjoy is Gary Soto's *Buried Onions* (1997), a story about a boy who is trying to escape the violence in the big city where he lives. Many of the boys in Linda's class can see themselves in the main character of this powerful story.

Question #7: Do the characters talk like you and your family do?

Frank was concerned because he could rarely find culturally relevant books that connected to his Arabic-speaking students. *Sitti's Secrets* (Nye, 1994) is a story about a girl living in the United States who goes to visit her grandmother in Palestine. The girl speaks only English, and her grandmother speaks only Arabic. However, both communicate through gestures and a few key Arabic words sprinkled throughout the text including *Sitti* (Grandmother), *habibi* (darling), and *mish-mish* (apricots). This touching story of the love between grandmothers and grandchildren especially connected to the Arabic-speaking students in the class, several of whom had grandparents living as far away as the grandmother in the story.

The Three Pigs/Los tres cerdos: Nacho, Tito, and Miguel (Salinas, 1998) served as an exciting shared reading for Manuel as he worked with a small group of struggling middle school Hispanic students. These boys immediately connected to the language of the characters and the detailed art in the book as well as the humorous characters and events. They noticed the details in the book, and one boy commented that Nacho's house looked like his *abuela*'s in Mexico. Another commented that the souped-up car looked like a *primo*'s (cousin's) car, and all noticed that the pigs liked to eat homemade *tortillas*. However, the students were most intrigued by the author's clever use of language to help readers connect to the book. In the first place, they appreciated the names of the three pigs—Nacho, Tito, and Miguel. One boy's nickname was actually Nacho and another had an Uncle Tito. They laughed that the wolf's name was José and the pigs said, "No way, José" when they wouldn't let him into their houses. Later in the story, the wolf drools hungrily imagining the *carnitas* and *chicharrones* (bits of braised pork and crisp pork rinds) he would eat once he caught the pigs. Familiar Spanish words such as these were sprinkled throughout the text. The boys even noticed that one pig, Miguel, had a bilingual T-shirt reading *"Leer es poder*: Reading is power." This familiar story connected to these readers because this version includes language, places, and events familiar to their own lives.

Question #8: How often do you read stories like these?

Recently, as an assignment for Yvonne's graduate class, students were asked to read a culturally relevant book to a student or group of students and administer the rubric. Yvette, a bilingual teacher, was appalled when the student she interviewed answered, *"Nunca"* (Never) to the question, "How often do you read stories like these?" *"¿Nunca?"* Yvette asked again. *"Nunca,"* her student insisted. Our concern is that many ELLs do not have access to culturally relevant books. Classroom libraries do not have enough books and certainly not enough in students' primary languages. Even when there are books in English or in students' native languages, few of those books have the characteristics that the culturally relevant rubric calls for: Few books are about the present experiences of the students, few books have characters that look like and talk like the students, few books have settings familiar to the students, and few books include the kinds of everyday experiences the students have had.

The power of using culturally relevant texts can be seen in the story related by another of Yvonne's graduate students. Suzanne is a monolingual teacher who had been concerned that her students, almost all of whom were Latinos, were not succeeding in reading and writing in English. At a state bilingual education conference, she bought many books, and nearly all had a Latino theme because she knew her classroom library had few books related to her students' backgrounds. Though she expected her students to connect with the books, she had no idea how exciting culturally relevant books would be for them.

She wrote about her experience of introducing one of these books to her students:

> "This afternoon I picked up *In My Family/En mi familia* by Carmen Lomas Garza (1996). Time being limited, my purpose was simply to show the new books I had bought to my fourth graders and to encourage them to investigate and enjoy the Spanish and English texts. The fever began as a slow burn as we discussed the wonderful cover illustration depicting an outdoor dance floor, people of all ages dancing, a musical ensemble, and simple light bulbs strung from posts. I asked my students what they thought of the cover and where they thought the dance was taking place. A roar went up. "MEXICO!"
>
> I decided to read a bit to see what sort of connections my students would make with the first short vignette described in the book, "The Horned Toads/Los camaleones." The room erupted in wild conversations during the reading. Students were unable to contain their excitement; they had stories to tell and, all decorum aside, they were going to tell them! They shared with their neighbors, friends, and, of course, me. They knew about horned toads, desert environments, and fire ants that "really sting." By the next vignette, "Cleaning Nopalitos/Limpiando nopalitos," there was no way to calm the wonderfully noisy groundswell of storytelling and sharing. I was entering their culture, a culture and tradition they were passionate to share" (D. Freeman & Y. Freeman, 2001, p. 109).

Suzanne's story illustrates the importance of using at least some culturally relevant texts. A few years ago, one might have argued that there were not many culturally relevant books available. However, now, at least for Hispanic students and especially those with Mexican origins, there are books that connect to students' lives and realities. Bilingual and ESL conferences at state and national levels display many such books from different cultures. Teachers can also find many culturally relevant books by searching online. Figure 4.4 lists the culturally relevant books referenced in this chapter.

Figure 4.4: **Culturally Relevant Books Bibliography**

Ada, A. F. (2002). *I love Saturdays y domingos*. New York: Atheneum Books.

Aliki. (1998). *Marianthe's story: Painted words and spoken memories*. New York: Greenwillow Books.

Anzaldúa, G. (1993). *Friends from the other side/Amigos del otro lado*. San Francisco: Children's Book Press.

Bunting, E. (1998). *Going home*. New York: HarperTrophy.

Choi, Y. (2001). *The name jar*. New York: Knopf.

del Castillo, R. G. (2002). *César Chávez: The struggle for justice/César Chávez: La lucha por la justicia*. Houston: Piñata Books.

Garza, C. L. (1996). *In my family/En mi familia*. San Francisco: Children's Book Press.

Jiménez, F. (2001). *Breaking through*. Boston: Houghton Mifflin.

Jiménez, F. (1997). *The circuit: Stories from the life of a migrant child*. Albuquerque, NM: University of New Mexico Press.

Jiménez, F. (1998). *La mariposa.* Boston: Houghton Mifflin.

Krull, K. (2003). *Harvesting hope: The story of César Chávez*. New York: Harcourt.

Nikola-Lisa, W. (1997). *America: My land, your land, our land*. New York: Lee & Low Books.

Nye, N. (1997). *Sitti's secret.* New York: Aladdin Paperbacks.

Palacios, A. (1997). *One city, one school, many foods*. Crystal Lake, IL: Rigby.

Paulsen, G. (1995a). *La tortillería* (G. d. A. Andújar, Trans.). Orlando, FL: Harcourt, Brace & Company.

Paulsen, G. (1995b). *The tortilla factory*. New York: Harcourt, Brace & Company.

Rodríguez, L. (1997). *América is her name*. Willimantic, CT: Curbstone Press.

Salinas, B. (1998). *The three pigs/Los tres cerdos: Nacho, Tito, and Miguel*. Oakland, CA: Piñata Publications.

Soto, G. (1997). *Buried onions*. San Diego, CA: Harcourt, Brace & Company.

Tsang, N. (2003). *Rice all day*. Barrington, IL: Rigby.

Freire (1987) summarized the importance of connecting what students read to their lives, and we as educators should not forget his words. Freire wrote: "Reading the world always precedes reading the word, and reading the word implies continually reading the world" (p. 35). The teachers we describe here have used culturally relevant books to ensure that their students always connect reading the word with reading their world.

Conclusion

When teachers understand the theory and research that support bilingual education, they implement practices that draw on students' primary languages and cultures even if the teachers do not speak the languages of their students. We have suggested a number of ways teachers can connect curriculum to students' lives. They can use preview/view/review; draw on cognates; and read culturally relevant books. When teachers follow practices like those described in this chapter, the ELLs in their classes become more engaged and experience greater academic success.

Applications for Chapter 4

1. In the chapter, we discussed three orientations toward language that have been seen in U.S. schools: language-as-a-handicap, language-as-a right, and language-as-a-resource. Interview four teachers working with ELLs and ask them about the importance and role of students' primary languages in school. From your interview, try to determine which orientation toward their students' first languages the teachers hold.

2. Cummins explains that when students develop knowledge and skills in their first language, they can transfer that knowledge to English because there is a common underlying proficiency (CUP). Interview a third-grade or older ELL student who is a recent arrival and doing well in school. Find out about his/her schooling in his or her first language. Also interview a struggling ELL student in third grade or above about his/her previous first-language schooling. What did you learn?

3. We describe ways that teachers can use preview/view/review in their teaching to help students understand content taught in English. Plan a short lesson in which you employ preview/view/review using ideas suggested in the text. Report on how the students responded to this experience.

4. The chapter provides ten tips for supporting students' first languages. Which of these do you already use in your classroom or have you seen used? Try implementing at least two of these ideas and report on how your ELLs respond.

5. Find a book that is culturally relevant for a group of ELL students you work with. Read the book to them and have them answer the questions on the Cultural Relevance Rubric (page 107) or conduct a discussion using the rubric as a guide. What did you learn from this experience?

6. Have you changed your views about bilingual education after reading this chapter? What questions do you still have?

CHAPTER 5

Emphasize Meaningful Reading and Writing

Plants and Seeds

Rosa is a first-grade teacher in a large city in Texas. Some of her students began school in pre-kindergarten as non-English speakers. Although the majority of her ELLs are native Spanish speakers, she also has students whose first languages include Arabic, Vietnamese, and Chinese. About half of her students are native English speakers. Rosa organizes her curriculum around themes and teaches language through content. She also draws on her students' primary languages and cultures. She knows that reading and writing taught with an emphasis on meaning-construction will help her ELLs learn both the English language and the key concepts they need in the content areas.

Science content fascinates her first graders and can be made comprehensible through visuals and hands-on activities. The science standards for her grade level include carrying out field investigations, asking questions, and drawing conclusions. In addition, students should be able to observe nature and identify and label living things in nature. Some of the language arts standards can be met through carefully planned science content instruction as well. For example, the language arts standards include reading both fiction and nonfiction, understanding the difference between fact and fiction, reading features of texts such as charts and graphs, participating in the reading of predictable books and poetry, and responding to readings through talk, art, music, and writing.

To meet these standards, Rosa and the other first-grade teachers decide to plan a unit on plant growth, answering questions such as "What makes a seed grow into a plant?" "What are the stages of plant growth?" and "How long do seeds take to grow into plants?" The teachers share activity ideas and put together a *text set* that supports a range of readers around this theme. During the unit, Rosa has her bilingual paraprofessional read the books that are available in Spanish to her Spanish-speaking ELLs as a preview to the English books.

Rosa starts her unit by bringing in a large jar filled with many different kinds of seeds. She shows the jar to the class, walking around the room so that

everyone can see what is in the jar. Then she asks, "What are these things in this jar?" Her students answer enthusiastically, "Seeds!" Then Rosa asks them if they can identify any of the seeds. Some children recognize corn; others recognize beans and pumpkin and watermelon seeds. Some children even recognize lettuce seeds and pepper seeds, explaining that they help their mothers plant those seeds in their family garden. Some of her ELLs know the names of the seeds in their native language and, as the English words are used, begin to pick up the new vocabulary.

Seed Growth

Next, Rosa reads three short picture books about seeds: *Plants and Seeds* (Walker, 1992a), *Seeds Grow* (Walker, 1992b), and *Plants Grow From Seeds* (Lucca, 2001). These limited-text books show different kinds of seeds and the plants that grow from the seeds, provide key content information, and are accessible for all her students, including her ELLs.

After reading and discussing the books, Rosa has the students form groups of four. They push their desks together, and she gives each group a plastic bag with a variety of seeds. She tells them to put together the seeds that are the same. The children group similar seeds and talk about the seeds as they work. When they are finished, Rosa puts a large piece of butcher paper on the wall. She draws a circle in the center and writes the word *seeds* in it. Then she asks the students if they can identify some of the seeds in their bag. She begins with one group. They know which are the bean seeds. Rosa draws a line from *seeds* and makes a smaller circle in which she writes *bean seeds*. Each group identifies one type of seed. The most difficult is the tiny carrot seed. As each group responds, Rosa adds to the web she has drawn.

Rosa then reads additional books about plant growth. The first book is *Growing Colors* (McMillan, 1988), a book of colorful photos showing various fruits and vegetables. The students and the teacher identify the plants and talk about shapes, colors, and textures. They decide, for example, that an orange is round, orange, and bumpy; an ear of corn is long and oval, yellow, and bumpy; and raspberries and blackberries are oval or round, red, black, and prickly. Rosa writes some of these descriptive words on the board.

Next, she hands out a blank chart with the word *seed* written at the top of the first column and the words *color*, *texture*, and *shape* heading the other columns. Working in their groups, the children examine their seeds again. They write the name of each type of seed on the chart and then fill in a description for each kind of seed. Students then share their descriptive words and Rosa adds the words to the web that she made earlier. This activity allows all of Rosa's students, including her ELLs, to categorize their seeds according to their characteristics using both familiar and new vocabulary.

Now that the students have started to develop vocabulary and concepts related to seeds, Rosa moves on to the topic of seed growth. She reads *Growing Radishes and Carrots* (Bolton & Snowball, 1985), a content pop-up book that contrasts how long it takes radishes and carrots to grow. This predictable text provides information on plant care. It also shows how plant growth can be measured and how much longer carrots take to grow than radishes. Rosa reminds her class about a story they read in kindergarten, *The Carrot Seed* (Krauss, 1945), and takes out the big-book version of the story. To help the children remember the story, Rosa shows the pictures and has the children tell her what is happening. Then she reads the book to the class, and students chime in at familiar places. This is the story of a boy who patiently waits for his carrot seed to grow. Rosa points out that it takes a long time for carrot seeds to grow, just as the nonfiction book she read earlier, *Growing Radishes and Carrots*, had explained.

The following day, Rosa takes out another big book, *Jessie's Flower* (Bacon, 1997). She and the students first discuss the cover, which shows a girl watching the ground where she had planted seeds. The students make some predictions about the story as Rosa does a picture walk through the book, turning the pages without reading the words. Rosa then reads the book, and the children discuss what these plants needed to grow, comparing them to *The Carrot Seed*.

The stories are quite similar. In each story there is a child who plants seeds and waits for the seeds to grow. However, there are also differences, so Rosa gives each group a paper with a Venn diagram drawn on it and asks the students to write how the stories are the same, where the circles intersect, and how they are different, on the two sides. When they finish, the groups share their responses with the class, and Rosa makes a composite Venn diagram on the overhead.

The next day, Rosa wants to review some of the key concepts the students have read about. During language arts, she and the students recite the poem "Growing" (Bogart, 1995), about a sunflower growing. She helps the students find the rhyming words. The class talks about how the poem describes what plants need to grow, something they have been studying in all of their readings. Then the students read a nonfiction limited-text book, *Sunflowers* (Boland, 1998b), which provides information about sunflowers, and a fiction text, *Sunflower House* (Bunting, 1996), which ends with the children in the story picking many, many seeds from the centers of their sunflowers. Rosa connects these books to another story about sunflowers, *Just One Seed* (Ada, 1990a), a pop-up big book in which the pop-up page shows a huge sunflower opening and the following page shows all the uses for sunflower seeds.

Another story that Rosa reads to the children is *I'm a Seed* (Marzollo, 1996), a story told from the point of view of two different seeds as they grow into plants. One is a flower and the other a pumpkin. The students discuss the steps of growth for each plant. They also discuss the differences between fact and fiction. The part of the story about how the plants grow contains facts, but the students recognize that since the seeds talk to each other, the story is partly fictional. Drawing on the information in all the books, Rosa and the students list the steps that are necessary to grow a plant from a seed. Then Rosa asks the students what they think their next project will be. "We're going to plant seeds and grow plants!" they guess.

Later that day, Rosa reminds the students that they are going to grow their own plants. She reads two books, *How Does It Grow?* (Morrison, 1998) and *Growing a Plant: A Journal* (Jenkins, 1998). The first book explains how a plant grows. It shows the steps for making seeds sprout. It also contains a description of an experiment students can do with plants to show root absorption. In addition, the book describes how to grow bean seeds. Rosa tells the students they will choose some seeds from their plastic bags and grow their own plants. Then Rosa reads the big-book version of *Growing a Plant: A Journal* and explains how they will keep a plant journal as their seeds grow. Rosa gives the students construction paper to make their journals.

During science time the next day, the students choose their seeds, dampen paper towels, wrap their seeds, and put them in plastic bags. Rosa has some groups put their seeds on a windowsill where they will get sun and has other groups put their seeds inside desks where it is dark. Still others place their seeds in the refrigerator in the classroom. Rosa tells the students that they will conduct an experiment to find out how these different conditions influence plant growth.

Over the next several days, students record in their plant journals the date and the number of days since the seeds were put into the wet paper towel. As the seeds sprout, the students draw pictures and label them to record the plant growth. As the plants grow, the students measure and graph them, comparing the growth in different environments: sun, dark, and cold. Rosa's students eventually transplant the healthy sprouts in dirt to watch them grow over the coming month.

Rosa's unit on plant growth helped her students develop both language and content. The students answered the questions, "What makes a seed grow into a plant?" "What are the stages of plant growth?" and "How long do seeds take to grow into plants?" They read and talked about texts of differing levels of difficulty that were connected by a common theme. Through reading these books they gained not only academic content but also the academic language they need for school. The students read fiction and nonfiction as well as poetry. They also read graphs and charts and kept their own plant journals. Throughout their theme study, the students were gaining knowledge and skills needed to meet the science and language arts standards and, at the same time, were becoming more proficient readers of English. Figure 5.1 lists the English and Spanish books Rosa used in her unit on plants and seeds.

Figure 5.1: **Plants and Seeds Unit Bibliography**

Ada, A. F. (1990a). *Just one seed*. Carmel, CA: Hampton-Brown.

Ada. A. F. (1990b). *Una semilla nada más*. Carmel, CA: Hampton-Brown.

Bacon, R. (1997). *Jessie's flower*. Crystal Lake, IL: Rigby.

Bogart, J. E. (1995). Growing. New York: Scholastic Inc.

Boland, J. (1998a). *Girasoles*. Katonah, NY: Richard C. Owen.

Boland, J. (1998b). *Sunflowers*. Katonah, NY: Richard C. Owen.

Bolton, F., & Snowball, D. (1985). *Growing radishes and carrots*. New York: Scholastic.

Bunting, E. (1996). *Sunflower house*. New York: Trumpet.

Jenkins, R. (1998). *Growing a plant: A journal*. Crystal Lake, IL: Rigby.

Krauss, R. (1945). *The carrot seed*. New York: Scholastic.

Krauss. R. (1978). *La semilla de zanahoria*. New York: Scholastic.

Lucca, M. (2001). *Plants grow from seeds*. Washington, DC: National Geographic Society.

Lucca, M. (2003). *De las semillas nacen las plantas*. Washington, DC: National Geographic Society.

Marzollo, J. (1996). *I'm a seed*. Carmel, CA: Hampton-Brown.

McMillan, B. (1988). *Growing colors*. New York: William Morrow & Co.

Morrison, R. (1998). *How does it grow?* Crystal Lake, IL: Rigby.

Walker, C. (1992a). *Plants and seeds*. Bothell, WA: The Wright Group.

Walker, C. (1992b). *Seeds grow*. Bothell, WA: The Wright Group.

Walker, C. (1995). *Plantas y semillas* (G. Andújar, Trans.). Bothell, WA: The Wright Group.

Meaningful Reading

English language learners face a real challenge in learning to read academic texts in English. Often, teachers are not sure of the best approach to help their students develop the necessary reading proficiency to succeed in school. In this chapter, we outline key concepts teachers should keep in mind as they plan literacy instruction for ELLs (D. Freeman & Y. Freeman, 2000; D. Freeman & Y. Freeman, 2004; Y. Freeman et al., 2005).

First, it is essential that teachers base their methods on a theory that views reading as constructing meaning. Too often, students reading in a second language learn to decode but fail to develop high levels of reading comprehension. Without good comprehension, they are not able to succeed academically. Second, effective teachers ensure that there is a good match between the theory they hold and the methods they use. In fact, the best way to assess a teacher's theory of reading is to observe the way in which he or she teaches literacy.

Goodman (1996) has developed a meaning-centered theory of reading based on extensive research with both native English speakers and ELLs. He has shown that proficient readers construct meaning from text by using their background knowledge and cues from three linguistic systems: graphophonics, syntax, and semantics. Goodman also explains that readers construct meaning by using a series of psychological strategies that include sampling, predicting, inferring, confirming or disconfirming, and integrating as they read. In the following sections we explain the importance of background knowledge, each of the cue systems, and the psychological strategies.

Background Knowledge

All readers apply what they know about the world to make sense of what they read. ELLs often lack the background needed to make sense of texts written in English because authors of these texts assume their readers all share certain cultural knowledge. For example, a writer might assume that all fifth graders know who George Washington was and what role he played in American history. They might also assume that their readers know about customs many families in the United States follow at Thanksgiving. However,

ELLs may never have been exposed to this information, so some texts are simply incomprehensible for them.

To get an idea of how difficult it is to understand a text without the needed background, read the following passage:

> *With hocked gems financing him our hero defied all scornful laughter that tried to prevent his scheme. "Your eyes deceive you," he had said, "an egg, not a table, correctly typifies this unexplored planet."*
>
> *Now three sturdy sisters sought proof, forging along, sometimes through calm vastness, yet more often over turbulent peaks and valleys. Days became weeks as many doubters spread fearful rumors about the edge. At last, from nowhere, welcome winged creatures appeared, signifying momentous success* (Dooling & Lachman, 1971).

If asked to explain what was meant by "an egg, not a table" or to identify the "three sturdy sisters," most readers would experience the same kind of difficulties many ELLs face when they lack the necessary background knowledge for their reading. Most readers of this chapter understand all the words. The problem is not with the vocabulary, but with the overall meaning. What would help is not improved decoding skills, but some building or activation of background knowledge. In fact, if we told you that this is a passage about Columbus' journey to America, most of you could explain the reference to "an egg" and name the "three sturdy sisters."

ELLs need background knowledge to comprehend English texts, and extensive reading of books at an appropriate level helps them build the needed knowledge. Teachers can also draw on their students' background knowledge and experiences by using books that are culturally relevant, as we explained in Chapter 4. These books allow ELLs to draw upon what they know as they build reading proficiency in English. To comprehend content area texts, ELLs also need a good academic knowledge base. A fifth-grade student will have trouble reading a grade-level science book if her science background is very limited. Building or activating background knowledge is the first step in helping students become proficient readers.

One way teachers can build background knowledge is to assemble *text sets*, as Rosa did. Text sets are groups of books organized around a particular topic. For example, the teacher might choose several books on weather during a theme study of "How does the weather affect our lives?" Text sets usually include both fiction and expository texts written at different levels of difficulty. Since students in any class represent a range of reading abilities, it is important to have books that challenge the best readers and other books that are accessible to the least-proficient readers. Assembling text sets on a topic ensures that all students will have access to books at their level.

Linguistic Cueing Systems

As they read, ELLs construct meaning from texts by using cues from three linguistic systems. Effective readers make a balanced use of all three systems. In the following sections, we explain each cue system.

Graphophonics

English is an alphabetic language. That means that the letters in words represent the sounds of the oral language. Readers use their knowledge of sounds and sound patterns, letters and letter patterns, and the relationships between sound patterns and letter patterns as they read. No written language provides a complete, one-to-one match between sounds and spellings. That is because writing systems represent meanings and word histories as well as sounds. For the most part, words in English are spelled the way they sound. However, some words are spelled to show the meaning connection between related words. For example, *bomb* is spelled with a silent *b*. The final *b* doesn't represent a sound, but it does show the relation between *bomb* and *bombard*. In the same way, *sign* has a silent *g*, but that *g* helps readers connect the related words, *sign* and *signal*. Both *medicine* and *medical* are spelled with *c*. The two *c*'s represent different sounds, but they provide a visual signal that these are related words. This connection would be lost if the spellings were *medisin* and *medical*.

If all words were spelled the way they sound, writing would be easier. Teachers could feel confident telling students to "spell it like it sounds." However, if all words were spelled the way they sound, reading would be harder. English has many homophones like *two, too,* and *to* or *one* and *won*.

Learning to use the right spelling for each word can be difficult at first, but the different spellings help readers assign the correct meaning to each word. If all English homophones were spelled the same, reading would be difficult. What would we make of a sentence like "Won buoy eight too pairs"? Isn't it easier to read and understand "One boy ate two pears"?

Other words are spelled to reflect their history. For example, in English the /k/ sound is usually spelled with a *c* when it is followed by a consonant or *a*, *o*, or *u*. Words like *kangaroo*, *koala*, and *kudos* should strike us as foreign-looking because they contain *k* where most English words have a *c*. The explanation for these unusual spellings is that these words are borrowed. When we borrow words, the original spellings are often retained. Rather than complaining that English spelling is a hopeless mess, teachers can encourage students to investigate word histories. When students learn that *kangaroo* is a word from an aboriginal Australian language, they usually also acquire the correct spelling.

The graphophonic system is largely acquired through exposure to meaningful texts, rather than learned through drills on sounds. Traditional phonics really doesn't work, especially for ELLs. There are too many rules and too many exceptions. Further, an English learner often uses a pronunciation that doesn't fit the rule. When teachers read aloud using big books, poems, and chants with large text that students can see, ELLs start to develop subconscious knowledge of the patterns of English spellings, and, at the same time, they begin to understand the meanings of English words. Students also benefit when teachers read alphabet books and engage students in creating alphabet books. In addition, students best develop a sense of the English spelling system as they are involved in language experience and shared writing activities. All these practices involve students in meaningful reading and writing.

During these activities, teachers may draw attention to certain sound and spelling patterns. For example, after reading a poem, the teacher might ask students to notice the different ways a certain sound is spelled. Teachers may also engage students in linguistic investigations to discover patterns of sound-spelling relationships. For example, a teacher could write the following pairs of words on the board: *rat rate*, *bit bite*, *rob robe*, and *cut cute*. Then the teacher might ask students to work in pairs to develop a rule that explains what happens when *e* is added to these words. Activities like these help students build a greater awareness of how English works. Students who are literate in their first language can also compare first-language spelling patterns with those in English. For example, a Spanish speaker might note that although English can start words with consonant blends such as *sp* and *st*, these combinations never appear at the beginning of Spanish words. In Spanish these consonant blends are preceded by *e*, as in *español*.

Syntax

The second linguistic cueing system is the syntactic system. Syntax refers generally to the order of words in a sentence. Word order is important in English because it signals meaning. In languages like Latin, the ending on a noun tells whether it is the subject or the object, so the order of the words can be changed with no change in meaning. However, in English, meaning is shown by word order. There is a big difference between "The teacher reprimanded the student" and "The student reprimanded the teacher."

In English, most clauses follow a pattern of actor, action, and object acted on. When we read, "The first little pig built his house of straw," we recognize that the first part of the sentence identifies who is doing something, the actor. The next part tells what he did, the action. And the third part tells who or what receives the action, the object of the verb. Even though sentences don't always follow this pattern, it is the most common pattern in English. Knowing the syntax at a subconscious level allows a reader to predict the kind of word that will come next. For example, if a sentence starts with "The," readers can predict with some confidence that the next word will be an adjective or a noun. If the sentence begins with "The teacher," readers predict that the next word will be a verb. Students familiar with English syntax also know that nouns follow prepositions, so when they read "He bought a jar of __," they can predict that the next word will be a noun telling what was in the jar.

English language learners acquire English syntax, both oral and written, by using English with a focus on meaning. As these students become more proficient, they can make better use of their developing knowledge of syntax to predict upcoming text. However, they can only do this if what they read is connected text that makes sense. Word lists do not help students develop the syntactic cueing system because lists lack syntax. As students become more proficient, they should be exposed to the more complex syntax found in academic texts, including sentences with several clauses and sentences written in passive form. It is only by gradually being exposed to more complicated syntax that students can begin to read and understand the academic English of school texts.

Semantics

The third linguistic cueing system is semantics. Semantics refers to word meanings. However, many words have several meanings. ELLs who only know that *fault* means "blame" will have difficulty reading a physical science text about *faults* in rocks. Not only are some words ambiguous, but the meaning of many words depends on knowledge of what the words refer to. For example, if students read, "Krashen supports FVR," they can only understand the sentence if they know who Krashen is and also know that FVR is an acronym for "free voluntary reading." ELLs often lack knowledge of what words refer to. In addition, ELLs often have trouble distinguishing between literal and nonliteral meanings. If a sentence reads, "He was a chicken," they may think that the character is actually an animal.

Knowledge of semantics also includes an understanding of what words go together. For example, in the following passage, the first few words alert a proficient reader that this text is about baseball, and the reader can predict that other baseball-related words will follow:

> The baseball *player* tossed his *bat* into the *dugout* after *striking out* for the third time. The *pitcher* really *had his number*. He took off his *spikes* and headed for the *locker room*, *cap* in hand.

Not only can a reader predict that many of the words will relate to baseball, but the meanings of several ambiguous words, such as *bat*, *pitcher*, and *dugout*, take on specific meanings because of the baseball context. The best way for ELLs to develop the semantic cueing system is extensive reading of different genres at an appropriate level of difficulty.

Interrelationship of Cueing Systems

The three cueing systems provide different kinds of knowledge that readers use to construct meaning. Graphophonic cues help readers recognize words. Syntactic cues help readers predict the kinds of words that will occur. Semantic cues help readers determine word meanings. The three systems work together. For example, in the passage on baseball, readers can use graphophonic cues from the letters and sounds of *player* to help recognize the word. Readers can use syntactic cues from the position of the word *player* following *The baseball* at the beginning of the sentence, which signals that it is a noun that serves as the subject or actor in the sentence. The semantic cues, including the context of baseball, help the reader assign the appropriate meaning to *player*. Cues from the three linguistic systems work together to help readers build meaning from texts.

Psychological Strategies

All readers also use a series of psychological strategies as they read. These are not consciously applied comprehension strategies. Instead, they are subconscious strategies that readers use naturally when they regard reading as a way to construct meaning from texts. The strategies used to make meaning from texts are the same as those used to make sense of oral language. The only difference is that the data for reading are visual and the data for oral language are acoustic.

Sampling

Readers begin by sampling a text. As their eyes move across a page, readers make short fixations on parts of words. When the eyes stop briefly to fixate text, information is sent to the brain. When the eyes are moving, no information is sent to the brain. Readers don't fixate every letter or even every word. Eye movement studies show that readers fixate about two-thirds of the words in a text (Paulson & Freeman, 2003). They use the information they gather to predict upcoming text.

Sampling is not the same as skimming and scanning, a conscious technique designed to help readers focus on important ideas in a passage. Rather, sampling is a subconscious process during which the brain directs the eyes to gather information needed to make sense of a passage. Some ELLs oversample. That is, they consciously slow down and begin to focus on each word in the text. They develop what Smith (1985) has termed "tunnel vision." The problem with reading too slowly is that the short-term memory is overloaded. By the time a student has finished reading a sentence or a paragraph, she can't remember how it started. ELLs don't need to become speed readers, but they do need to move through a text rapidly enough to avoid memory overload.

Predicting and Inferring

As they sample a text, readers continually predict words, sentences, and longer passages. Readers of English obtain most of their information about words using graphophonic cues from the first and last letters along with syntactic and semantic cues. For example, after reading "The player tossed his" in the baseball passage, a reader might use her knowledge of syntax to predict that the next word might be a noun specifying what the player tossed. Using semantic cues, the reader would predict that a baseball player might toss a bat, ball, or glove. Then, using graphophonic cues supplied by the first and last letters, *b__t*, the reader could fill in the word *bat*. In order to make word, sentence, or text-level predictions, ELLs need background knowledge. In this case, they need to know about the game of baseball. And they need to use cues from all three linguistic systems.

Readers also make inferences. Eye-movement studies reveal that readers fixate on content words (nouns, verbs, adjectives, and adverbs) more than function words (preposition, conjunctions, articles). This is because the brain directs the eyes to pick up the most relevant information. The process works efficiently because the focus on key words allows a reader to keep reading at a fast-enough rate to avoid memory overload. However, the process works only if the reader can infer or fill in the missing information. Inference operates primarily at the text level. The author doesn't say that there was an umpire or fans. Readers must use their knowledge of baseball to fill in these details. Often ELLs lack background knowledge on topics such as American sports or U.S. history. However, as ELLs read more with a focus on meaning, they begin to build the background they need to comprehend increasingly difficult texts. This is true for both fiction and expository texts.

Confirming or Disconfirming and Integrating

As reading continues, proficient readers constantly check to confirm their predictions. They monitor to see if the passage is still making sense. If the prediction is confirmed, the reader can continue. However, if something occurs later in the text to disconfirm the prediction, a proficient reader will go back and reread. For example, a reader of the baseball passage might predict that the sentence would read, "The baseball player tossed his ball into the dugout after striking out for the third time" and then realize that a player who strikes out has a bat, not a ball. The word *ball* doesn't make sense, so the reader goes back and rereads the passage to correct the miscue.

As readers sample a text, make predictions and inferences, and confirm or disconfirm and correct, they continually integrate new knowledge with the meaning they have been building. The process is cyclical and operates very rapidly. Readers continually sample, predict, infer, confirm or disconfirm, and integrate, using cues from the three linguistic cueing systems as they progress through a text. The process works well as long as the reader stays focused on meaning.

Reading—A Universal Process

Goodman (1996) claims that the process readers use to make sense of text is a universal process. Whether students are reading in Spanish or Chinese, they use their background knowledge and the same linguistic cueing systems and psychological strategies. All languages, despite their surface differences, use symbols to represent meanings. Chinese characters, for the most part, do not provide sound cues the way English letters do, but readers of Chinese use visual information as they read. In Japanese the verb comes at the end of the sentence rather than following the subject, but Japanese writing follows predictable syntactic patterns. Written words and characters refer to people, things, and actions no matter what the language, so readers of any language use semantic cues along with syntactic and graphic or graphophonic cues.

In addition, readers of any language use the same psychological strategies to construct meaning from text. All readers need to sample, predict, infer, confirm or disconfirm, and integrate information. The process is the same because the human brain is the same, no matter what the language. Since reading is a universal process, the method of teaching reading should also be the same, whether the student is learning to read Arabic, Russian, or English.

The universality of the reading process helps explain why ELLs with adequate formal schooling who are literate in their first language learn to read in English more rapidly than students who are not literate in their first language. Students with first-language literacy still have to figure out how the new language works, but they can transfer to English many of the skills they use to read in their first language.

Even though there may be differences between the syntactic structures and the graphophonic systems of the two languages, these literate students bring important knowledge and skills to reading in English. They already know that reading should make sense and that they should apply their background knowledge as they read. They also know, at least subconsciously, that texts offer cues from three linguistic systems and that they can apply the same psychological strategies when they read in English that they rely on when reading in their first language. Students who are literate in their first language benefit when teachers keep the focus on meaning. This focus allows them to draw on the skills and strategies they have already developed. ELLs also benefit when teachers use strategies to help them transfer first-language reading skills to English. For example, teachers can help students make predictions or draw on cognates as they read in English.

All ELLs also face a number of challenges as they read in a new language. They need to acquire new sound-to-letter correspondences and new syntactic patterns. They also need to develop an extensive English academic vocabulary, and this is best accomplished through reading complete texts. Students who don't already read in their first language need to develop both oral and written English. They can best learn these two forms of language at the same time. In fact, there is simply not enough time to insist that students master oral language before tackling reading. As teachers engage them with progressively more difficult texts, ELLs develop important academic concepts and academic vocabulary in each of the content areas.

Supporting the Development of Reading for ELLs

Krashen (2004) argues that reading is acquired in the same way as oral language, through receiving comprehensible input. For literacy development, the input must be in written form. Teachers make written input comprehensible by choosing culturally relevant texts and by building background knowledge. Written input is also more comprehensible if the texts teachers choose and the strategies they use scaffold instruction for ELLs.

Characteristics of Texts

In addition to using culturally relevant texts, teachers should also choose books that have characteristics that support ELL readers. Figure 5.2 lists characteristics of text that support meaning construction. Below we discuss each characteristic on the checklist.

Authentic texts that contain natural language support meaning construction for ELLs. Some school texts are written to teach a certain letter-sound correspondence. For example, a story might have many words with a short-*a* sound. The books are designed to help students practice this phonics pattern. A text such as "The fat cat sat on a mat" is not interesting or informative. Authors usually focus on their message, not on using words with a certain sound. Further, the language that results is not natural, and research (Kucer & Tuten, 2003) has shown that texts written with natural language are easier to read than simplified texts. Simplified texts often contain short sentences and unnatural syntax. These texts do not prepare ELLs for the reading they will do in mainstream classes.

Prediction is one of the psychological strategies that all readers use, so predictable books offer support for meaning construction. Books for beginning readers often include a repeated phrase or rhyming words, and these devices make the text easier to predict. Books are also more predictable when students are familiar with the patterns of different genres. Stories, for example, usually follow a problem-solution pattern whereas expository texts may have a main idea and supporting details. For this reason, it is important to engage ELLs with texts from different genres and to point out the patterns in the different kinds of texts.

Figure 5.2: **Checklist for Characteristics of Texts
That Support Meaning Construction**

---

1. Are the materials authentic? Authentic materials are written to inform or entertain, not to teach a grammar point or a letter-sound correspondence.

2. Is the language of the text natural? When there are only a few words on a page, do these limited-text books sound like real language, something people really say?

3. Is the text predictable? Books are more predictable when students have background knowledge of the concepts, so teachers should activate or build background.

> **For emergent readers:**
> Books are more predictable when they follow certain patterns (repetitive, cumulative) or include certain devices (rhyme, rhythm, alliteration).
>
> **For developing readers:**
> Books are more predictable when students are familiar with text structures (beginning, middle, end; problem-solution; main idea, details, examples, etc.).
>
> Books are more predictable when students are familiar with text features (headings, subheadings, maps, labels, graphs, tables, indexes).

4. Is there a good text-picture match? A good match provides nonlinguistic visual cues. Is the placement of the pictures predictable?

5. Are the materials interesting and/or imaginative? Interesting, imaginative texts engage students.

Considerations for Older English Language Learners

6. Is the text limited?

7. Is the content age-appropriate?

8. Are the pictures, photographs, or other art appropriate for older students?

Pictures, illustrations, and other visual elements support ELLs in their reading. When students lack the linguistic resources to comprehend a text fully, they can rely on these nonlinguistic supports. Above all, stories and expository texts should be interesting. When students are interested in a story or an informational text, they are motivated to understand what they are reading. Often, ELLs will tackle a difficult book because they really want to read it.

Two other considerations should be added for older ELLs. First, if students struggle to read, then the text should be limited. Second, the content should be age-appropriate, but if there are too many words on a page, some students become discouraged. Poetry is a good choice for older ELLs. Poems have fewer words than stories, but they often deal with topics students find interesting. In addition, magazines on topics ELLs are interested in are a good resource. Third, older readers are more engaged when pictures and illustrations are age-appropriate. Books with pictures of young children send the wrong message to older students.

Gradual Release of Responsibility

Once teachers choose appropriate reading materials, they can scaffold their instruction to help ELLs develop the skills they need. Effective instruction follows a gradual release of responsibility model (Pearson & Gallagher, 1983). If students are not able to read in English, teachers need to do the reading for them. At first, teachers read aloud to students and engage them in discussion of what was read. This helps ELLs develop background and the language of books.

Next, teachers read with students during shared reading, often using books with enlarged print so all the students can follow along and acquire letter-sound correspondences, fluency, and English syntactic patterns and semantic knowledge. During shared reading, ELLs may chime in on repeated passages. The responsibility for reading is still primarily with the teacher, but students now take on some responsibility as well. Teachers may also pair students to read together. Often a more proficient English speaker will be paired with one who is less proficient.

Following shared reading, teachers work with small groups of students in guided reading sessions during which they focus on specific skills students need to acquire. During this small-group instruction, ELLs may read a passage or a small book with support from the teacher. The responsibility is gradually shifting from the teacher to the students. Finally, ELLs apply the skills they develop in shared and guided reading as they read independently. With more difficult texts or new genres, teachers often repeat the process of reading aloud, shared reading, guided reading, and independent reading. The gradual release of responsibility model allows teachers to scaffold reading and teach ELLs the skills they need to read independently.

The theory of reading we have outlined here has three key components: background knowledge, linguistic cues, and psychological strategies. When teachers have a clear understanding of this meaning-centered theory of reading and use materials and teaching methods consistent with the theory, they enable their ELLs to develop the knowledge and skills they need to make sense of English texts and succeed academically. We conclude this chapter with an example from a sixth-grade teacher who helps his students become more proficient readers through meaningful content instruction.

Nutrition Unit

Richard is a sixth-grade teacher at a school in a rural farming community in New Mexico where his Mexican-origin students, who began school speaking Spanish and have been transitioned, now receive their daily content and literacy instruction in English. In addition, some of his students are native English speakers. Students come to him with differing levels of reading proficiency in English. Richard works hard at planning curriculum that will lead his students to academic success. He understands that literacy skills and content knowledge developed in the first language transfer to the second language (Cummins, 2000; Krashen, 2004). However, he is aware that many of his ELLs never developed literacy at grade level in Spanish. The majority of his students are long-term English learners who speak English well but struggle with reading and writing in English. Some students are newer to this country and do read and write in Spanish, although they have not fully developed conversational English. Richard makes Spanish versions of the English books in his units available to these students whenever possible. Richard wants to help all his students to read, write, and learn academic content in English because he knows this is critical for their future academic success.

Richard makes literacy development the keystone of his curriculum. As he plans his lessons, Richard uses the gradual release of responsibility model as a guide. If students are not able to read in English, Richard understands that he needs to do the reading for them at first. Then, he reads with them, has them read together in pairs, and works with them in guided reading groups to help them develop good reading strategies. His goal is for his students to read independently.

In addition to providing his students with many opportunities to read, Richard organizes his curriculum around content themes that draw on the standards and his students' background knowledge and interests. His unit on nutrition is an example of how he carefully chooses culturally relevant materials and topics organized around big questions to help his students develop academic concepts and literacy.

Richard reviewed the social studies, health, math, and language arts standards as he planned this theme. He incorporated social studies standards in economics that require students to compare ways in which various societies organize the production and distribution of goods and require them to identify and differentiate among traditional, market, and command economies in selected contemporary societies. In math he worked on estimation with his students, and in health education he focused on standards that called for students to analyze healthful and unhealthful dietary practices. The language arts standards call for students to compare and contrast texts from different genres, to paraphrase and summarize texts and organize ideas, to draw inferences using text evidence and experience, and to draw on background knowledge to interpret readings. To meet these standards and to encourage his students to read extensively, Richard provides his students with books at differing levels of difficulty around the theme. His text set on nutrition includes many books that also have a version in Spanish. Students who are stronger readers in Spanish then can read the books in English but also can refer to the versions in Spanish to help support their reading comprehension.

To introduce the unit and to encourage students to begin talking about the topic of the food traditions of different cultures, Richard poses the big questions, "How do traditional foods from around the world compare with our foods?" and "Which of the traditional foods are nutritious?" Next, he reads *Everyone Cooks Rice* (Dooley, 1991) to his class. In this book the main characters go from house to house, and in each home they are served rice prepared in the style unique to a particular culture. Drawing on this story, Richard divides his students into groups. Each group chooses one section of the story and reports on the special rice preparation described in that section. This activity stimulates lively discussion and leads students to talk about their own family's favorite rice dishes.

As the discussion progresses, students begin to express their food preferences. This provides an excellent opportunity for Richard to take out *Judge for a*

Day (González-Jensen, 1997b), a story about an Anglo boy who hesitates to judge Latino dishes in an international food festival because he doesn't like spicy food. The story dispels the myth that all Hispanics are alike and that all Hispanic food is spicy. It encourages students to be adventurous eaters and to appreciate the variety of foods that different countries have to offer. Since Richard has multiple copies of this book, he pairs more proficient readers with struggling readers so they can help one another.

Richard then asks his students to brainstorm questions they might use to interview one another about their food preferences. The students ask one another about the foods they like and don't like. Richard lists the class preferences on the board and shows them how to make a bar graph to illustrate the results.

In addition to graphing, Richard also wants students to work on estimation. He has multiple copies of the book *That's About Right: A Book About Estimating* (Burke, 2004). He puts his students into groups to read about estimating. Then each group chooses a favorite food and estimates how much of each ingredient they would need if they were going to cook the dish for the entire class. The next day, Richard brings in newspaper ads from local grocery stores, and students first estimate and then calculate how much money they would need to buy the ingredients for their favorite dish. Students conclude that feeding the whole class would cost quite a lot of money. They compare and contrast which groups had the most expensive dishes and decide which ingredients were the most expensive. They discover, for example, that dishes without meat often are not as expensive as dishes calling for meat.

Richard reads *Saturday Sancocho* (Torres, 1995b), a book about a traditional Central and South American stew. He then asks his students if they have ever eaten a dish like *sancocho*. Some students explain that their families prepare a similar dish, but it doesn't have yucca or *plátano verde* (green plantains) in it. They enthusiastically describe the ingredients and preparation of stews and soups their relatives serve, including typical Mexican stews such as *posole* and *menudo*.

Saturday Sancocho brings up a social studies topic for Richard and his students to discuss. In the story, María Lili and her grandparents, who traditionally have *sancocho* on Saturdays, have a dozen eggs but no money. María Lili and her grandmother go to the market, and through some clever bargaining and trading, end the afternoon with all the ingredients they need for *sancocho*, including a chicken. Richard asks his students if they could do what the characters in the story did here in the United States with no money, only something to trade. Some students bring up experiences they had bartering in Mexico with relatives at the market or in small villages, but all agree that in this country, this would not happen. This discussion of differences leads the class to the topic of immigration.

Richard has the students move into groups to read three different books related to this discussion, *Mexican Immigration* (Pile, 2005), *To Trade or Not to Trade* (Hirsch, 2004), and *Golden Opportunities* (2004). He asks the students reading *Mexican Immigration* to find out why Mexican immigrants came to this country and what they found here. The students reading *To Trade or Not to Trade* are asked to trace the history of economics in this country from early bartering to present-day trade industries. The group reading *Golden Opportunities* is asked to find specific examples of new immigrants who became entrepreneurs in this country by taking advantage of the free-enterprise system.

After gathering the information, each group prepares a short PowerPoint presentation to share with the whole class. As each group makes their presentation, the class engages in discussion of the topic. The presentation on *Golden Opportunities* leads several students to tell how their families had started little businesses including a restaurant, a shoe-repair shop, and a bakery in this country. Others tell how their families dream of having their own business.

The next day during language arts Richard reminds his students of *Saturday Sancocho* and then reads the English portion of the bilingual book *Sip, Slurp, Soup, Soup, Caldo, Caldo, Caldo* (Gonzales-Bertrand, 1996), which describes the preparation of a delicious soup and the ingredients that go into it. Some of the students comment that they don't like some of the ingredients that go into the soup. Together the class lists the ingredients described in the book, and then Richard asks his students to write a list of the ingredients that they would have asked their mothers to leave out. After each student has made a list, Richard leads the class to compile a list to see whether there would be any ingredients left in their soup once they took out the ingredients that different class members didn't like!

Next, Richard introduces a math activity by showing the students a poem he has put on a large poster, "In the Mood for a Favorite Food" (Merriam, 1995). The students then brainstorm a list of their favorite foods, referring to the graph they made earlier. Pizza comes up as the class favorite. Richard distributes copies of *Making Pizza With Math* (Shulman, 2004). Students then work in pairs to practice reading the interview questions in the book. One student takes the role of a student and the other the pizza maker. After students have practiced, some pairs volunteer to read the interview aloud. Following this, the entire class talks about the different ways that estimating is used in making pizza: in measuring ingredients, in weighing dough, and in figuring prices of different size pizzas. The book ends with the pizza being cut up to be eaten, and Richard asks the students what fraction of the pizza each of them would like. When students seem to hesitate, he reads them another book, *Eating Fractions* (McMillan, 1991). Then the class works together to determine what fraction of a pizza each student would get if it were divided equally.

Because he wants to move into a discussion of the food pyramid and because spaghetti often comes up as a favorite food, Richard projects a transparency of "Spaghetti! Spaghetti!" (Prelutsky, 1996) and leads the students in a spirited reading of this humorous poem. During free-choice reading time, some students locate two more poems about pasta from *What's on the Menu?* (Goldstein, 1995), "Italian Noodles" (Kennedy, 1995) and "Ready for Spaghetti" (Guthard, 1995). Several students ask Richard if they can use some of these food poems for the poetry festival that will take place the following month. The class decides that food poems will be their presentation theme.

Richard takes out a large poster of the food pyramid. He asks students to look at the pyramid, talk together in pairs, and then tell him what they notice.

Students comment that "you should eat lots of bread and pasta," but "you shouldn't eat too much greasy or sweet stuff." Richard then asks the students to think about spaghetti, rice, and traditional dishes like *sancocho*, *posole*, and *caldo* and decide if they are nutritious or not. Students note that all the dishes include different sections of the food pyramid. Several students add that they eat bread or tortillas with their *caldo* or spaghetti so they are getting plenty of cereals and pastas.

The next morning, Richard reviews the food pyramid and then takes four items from a paper bag: a flour tortilla, a corn tortilla, a hamburger bun, and a bagel. He asks students to compare and contrast the four kinds of breads. Students working in groups list the differences and similarities, including characteristics such as size, shape, ingredients, and taste. Richard then puts up a poster, "Los panes del mundo" (Breads Around the World) (1993), and students discuss how people all over the world eat some kind of bread. Students notice that many breads look like the Mexican *pan dulce* (pastries). Richard takes advantage of this interest by reading and discussing *From Father to Son* (Almada, 1997b), a nonfiction story of a family bakery business in Los Angeles where wonderful "*ricos pasteles y toda clase de pan dulce*" (delicious cakes and all types of pastries) are produced.

The culmination of this comparison comes when Richard asks his Mexican-origin students what bread is their favorite. Despite the fact that they all love *pan dulce*, they all say, "Tortillas!" especially those just off the griddle, made by their mothers or grandmothers. Since he wants to draw on their Mexican roots, Richard reads *Mexico's Marvelous Corn* (González-Jensen, 1997b), which tells how corn is processed to make many typical Mexican foods including *tamales*, *atole*, and, of course, tortillas. He also reads *The Tortilla Factory* (Paulsen, 1995b), a cycle book that moves from planting the corn to growing it, to harvesting it, to making corn flour, to making tortillas with the flour, and then to eating it to give energy to plant more corn. Both of these books encourage discussion, and students eagerly write about their experiences planting and harvesting corn, visiting tortillerías, or making their favorite dishes with tortillas.

Richard concludes this section of his unit by reading *A Spoon for Every Bite* (Hayes, 2005), a humorous folktale about poor Mexicans who tell their rich neighbor that they know someone who uses a different spoon for every bite of food. The rich man goes broke trying to buy enough spoons to keep up with this mysterious person, and, in the end, he finds out that the spoon the Mexicans are referring to is a tortilla. Many Mexicans use tortillas to scoop up food and with each bite, they use a different part of the "spoon." Richard's students thoroughly enjoy this folktale.

In the afternoon, Richard continues with the nutrition theme. He reads *Bread, Bread, Bread* (Morris, 1989), a book about breads all over the world. Students are interested to see different shapes of loaves of bread, tortillas, French bread, and even pretzels and pizza among the photographs of breads eaten around the world. They compare the breads in this book to the breads they had discussed that morning.

Richard's goal for this discussion of the different kinds of bread people eat is to have his students begin to understand the value of their own eating customs and those of others. To enhance the discussion about different eating customs around the world, the class reads *Bread Is for Eating* (Gershator & Gershator, 1995), *Good Morning, Let's Eat* (Badt, 1994), and *Pass the Bread* (Badt, 1995), books rich in photographs that tell about breads around the world and what people all over the world eat for breakfast. To extend the nutrition unit to social studies, the students work together in small groups to locate on the world map where the people live who eat the different breakfasts and breads. They also discuss how where people live affects what can be easily grown and purchased and how that influences the types of foods people eat.

Richard ends the unit by turning to the kinds of foods that are representative of his students' own Latino backgrounds and reads *Chato's Kitchen* (Soto, 1995), a book all his students love. Besides listing the traditional Mexican foods the "cool cats" from the barrio prepare to try to trick the mice at their dinner, the students discuss the nutritional value of the dishes served by the mice and decide that the dishes are, indeed, very good for their health. Figure 5.3 lists the books in English and Spanish that Richard used during the nutrition unit.

Figure 5.3: **Nutrition Unit Bibliography**

Almada, P. (1997a). *Del padre al hijo*. Crystal Lake, IL: Rigby.

Almada, P. (1997b). *From father to son*. Crystal Lake, IL: Rigby.

Badt, K. (1994). *Good morning, let's eat*. Chicago: Children's Press.

Badt, K. (1995). *Pass the bread*. Chicago: Children's Press.

Burke, M. B. (2004). *That's about right: A book about estimating*. Barrington, IL: Rigby.

Dooley, N. (1991). *Everyone cooks rice*. New York: Carolrhoda Books, Inc.

Gershator, D., & Gershator, P. (1995). *Bread is for eating*. New York: Scholastic.

Golden opportunities. (2004). Barrington, IL: Rigby.

Goldstein, B. S. (Ed.). (1995). *What's on the menu?* New York: Puffin Books.

Gonzales-Bertrand, D. (1996). *Sip, slurp, soup, soup, caldo, caldo, caldo*. Houston: Piñata Books.

González-Jensen, M. (1997a). *El maíz maravilloso de México*. Crystal Lake, IL: Rigby.

González-Jensen, M. (1997b). *Judge for a day*. Crystal Lake, IL: Rigby.

González-Jensen, M. (1997c). *Juez por un día*. Crystal Lake, IL: Rigby.

González-Jensen, M. (1997d). *Mexico's marvelous corn*. Crystal Lake, IL: Rigby.

Guthard, P. (1995). Ready for spaghetti. In B. Goldstein (Ed.), *What's on the menu?* (p. 13). New York: Puffin Books.

Hayes, J. (2005). *A spoon for every bite/Una cuchara para cada bocado*. El Paso: Cinco Puntos Press.

Hirsch, C. F. (2004). *To trade or not to trade*. Barrington, IL: Rigby.

Kennedy, X. J. (1995). Italian noodles. In B. Goldstein (Ed.), *What's on the menu?* (p. 12). New York: Puffin Books.

Los panes del mundo. (1993). New York: Scholastic.

McMillan, B. (1991). *Eating fractions*. New York: Scholastic.

Merriam, E. (1995). In the mood for a favorite food. In B. Goldstein (Ed.), *What's on the menu?* (p. 10). New York: Puffin Books.

Morris, A. (1989). *Bread, bread, bread*. New York: Mulberry Books.

Paulsen, G. (1995a) *La tortílleria*. Orlando, FL: Harcourt Brace & Company.

Paulsen, G. (1995b) *The Tortilla Factory*. Orlando, FL: Harcourt Brace & Company.

Pile, M. (2005). *Mexican immigration*. Washington, DC: National Geographic.

Prelutsky, J. (1996). Spaghetti! Spaghetti! In J. D. Cooper & J. J. Pikulski (Eds.), *Celebrate*. Boston: Houghton Mifflin.

Shulman, L. (2004). *Making pizza with math*. Barrington, IL: Rigby.

Soto, G. (1995). *Chato's kitchen*. New York: Scholastic.

Torres, L. (1995a). *El sancocho del sábado*. New York: Farrar, Straus and Giroux.

Torres, L. (1995b). *Saturday sancocho*. New York: Farrar, Straus and Giroux.

Richard chose a content theme of interest to his students and books that would draw on his students' cultural backgrounds. By reading a variety of books including fiction, nonfiction, and poetry around the same theme, Richard's students built up their English academic language related to foods, food origins, food preparation, and geography. The students increased their content knowledge in the areas of economics, health, math, and social studies. Throughout the unit, Richard provided books at different levels of difficulty. In this way, all the students were able to have success with reading. Perhaps the greatest benefit of the unit for Richard's students was that they came to appreciate their own cultural tradition as well as the traditions of other cultural groups.

Applications for Chapter 5

1. In this chapter we emphasize meaningful reading and we discuss the three cue systems that readers use as they construct meaning from text. Review these three systems and be prepared to explain them to a partner.

2. Readers use psychological strategies when they read. What are those strategies and how do they work? Share with a partner and write down questions you and your partner have.

3. One way to ensure that reading is meaningful is to organize books into text sets that support thematic instruction. Consider a thematic unit that you are teaching or have taught. Put together at least five fiction and five nonfiction books that would support that theme. Bring those books to class to share in small groups.

4. When choosing appropriate books to support students' reading, it is helpful to refer to the Checklist for Characteristics of Texts That Support Meaning Construction (page 135). Choose a book that you think has some of the characteristics listed on the checklist. Bring that book to class and be prepared to share it in a small group, explaining how it meets the criteria listed in the checklist.

5. Review Rosa's theme on plants and seeds and Richard's theme on nutrition. How did each of these teachers ensure that their students viewed reading as meaningful? Be specific as you explain the activities that students were involved with and the books that the students read.

CHAPTER 6

Develop Academic Language

We concluded Chapter 3 with a description of part of Mary's high school unit on the topic of sense of self. The students in Mary's regular English classes as well as her ESL students were involved in various projects including interviewing one another, making a coat of arms, writing an "I Am" poem and an Autobiopoem, and completing a "Here's Looking at You" questionnaire. Through these activities, students built their descriptive vocabulary and their ability to write complete paragraphs.

Mary knew her students needed to continue to develop their writing ability. In order to help them do this, she planned both writing and reading activities to draw on their experiences and build important background knowledge. Since one standard for ninth-grade language arts requires students to demonstrate the ability to relate a sequence of events and communicate the significance of the events, Mary involved her students in activities that would enable them to complete this kind of writing.

First, she asked her students to think about the good things and the bad things that had happened to them during their lives. She modeled how to make a list of good and bad events, giving examples from her own life. Then she asked her students to make their own lists. After they had written their lists, she demonstrated on the board how she would like them to evaluate those experiences and graph their list on a scale. She listed her own experiences and gave each one a number from –5 (the worst thing) to +5 (the best thing). Then she asked students to evaluate their lists. Students had to decide how negative or how positive each of the events was. For example, Monica graphed "My third-grade teacher got me into reading" as a +4.5, and "I got a poem published!" as a +5, but "I have a lost uncle" as –5 and "Three of my best friends moved away" as –4.5.

Later, during the daily reading and discussion time, Mary connected the students' life highs and lows to another activity. She had students read several newspaper articles that described personal experiences. In one, a Hispanic teenager remembered how he was teased as a fourth grader because he was fat. His descriptive writing earned him second place in the local newspaper's teen writing contest. In another, two boys described how they felt about an encounter with a homeless man. Mary and her students looked together at the descriptive language in the articles and discussed how the authors helped readers feel the experience by the way they wrote. Each student then picked one of the high or low points in his or her life and wrote about his or her personal experience, trying to be as descriptive as the authors of the articles.

As Mary continued with the unit, she connected activities to more of the writing standards as well as standards that her students needed to meet in reading. For example, the writing standards call for students to write in

a voice and style appropriate for the audience, to learn to use figurative language, to apply meanings of prefixes, suffixes, and roots to comprehend what they read, to use the dictionary and other reference materials, and to monitor their reading strategies. The standards also require that students summarize, identify main ideas and supporting details, analyze the relevance of setting and time, analyze characters and point of view, identify conflicts, and analyze the development of plot. Mary planned different reading and writing activities to include these standards as she further developed the sense-of-self unit.

The "Four Skinny Trees" chapter of Sandra Cisneros' powerful book *The House on Mango Street* (Cisneros, 1984) provided Mary with an opportunity to help her students with metaphor. In "Four Skinny Trees" Cisneros compares herself to four trees growing outside her bedroom window. The students discussed the concept of voice and how the author expressed her voice in this chapter. After reading and discussion, students chose some kind of plant, animal, or object that represented them. They first drew what they had chosen and then wrote about themselves using figurative language, such as metaphors, when possible.

Next, Mary asked the students to chart significant events in their lives, listing each event, descriptive words to describe the event, and the person most associated with the event. Students referred to their earlier lists as they completed the chart. From this list of significant events, the students picked one event. Their next assignment was to make a personal narrative map. Mary showed them a sample map. It had boxes in which students were to elaborate on the event they had chosen by listing the setting, the characters, the problem, the solution, and the beginning, middle, and end.

José, who is in Mary's ESL 1 class, showed that he understood the concept of problem when he wrote in that box, "I don't understand to the art teacher" and in the solution box, "A friend Raul translate to me. Then I understand everything." Once students filled in their narrative maps, Mary had them work in pairs to review each other's papers. The reviewer answered a series of questions including: What will the story be about? What do you think will be interesting? What details not on the personal narrative map would you like to know? Which character seems most interesting? What might be a title for the story? This peer evaluation helped the writers see if their details were clear before they started to write.

To ensure that the students read their peer's evaluations, the students themselves had to respond to their reviewer's comments on another sheet, answering questions such as these: Did the reviewers understand what your story would be about? What did they think would be interesting? What details did they want to know? Which was their favorite character? Did you like the title ideas your peers provided?

All of the scaffolding activities Mary provided helped her students understand the elements they should include in their writing. However, Mary realized that students also needed models from proficient writers. She knew that reading provides the best background possible for writers. She had read the works of Krashen (2004), who explains there is overwhelming research evidence showing that reading is the major way we develop vocabulary, spelling, grammatical competence, and writing style.

Because many of her students were migrant students or had families who worked in agriculture, Mary decided to have the students read and respond to the personal experiences of the migrant child in *The Circuit* (F. Jiménez, 1997). Mary wanted to use this book to teach some key concepts called for in the standards, including finding textual evidence to support opinions, using reference materials, and using reading strategies. She also planned to teach literary terms including *tone, allusion, flashback, symbol,* and *foreshadowing,* which are called for in the standards.

Mary first gave the students a sheet titled "Reading Strategies." She then lectured on some strategies they could use before and during reading to figure out words they didn't know. These strategies were to use context, dictionaries and glossaries, and prefixes, roots, and suffixes. Students took notes on a sheet she gave them with a section for each of these strategies. In this process, Mary helped her students understand how to take notes by writing down key information they would need later. On another day, she gave them a sheet on summarizing. Again, students took notes on the definitions of *summary* and *gist* with examples of each.

To reinforce literary terms such as *tone, setting, story elements, characters, allusion, flashback, symbol, foreshadowing,* and *theme,* Mary worked with her students in the large group, discussing examples from *The Circuit,* and then had students work in pairs, giving them photocopied sections of the text. For example, students worked together to find examples of allusion to famous Mexican heroes and flashbacks to earlier childhood experiences in the story. They cut out these examples and pasted them on a large sheet of butcher paper, and they shared them with the entire group.

The students also practiced finding textual evidence to support key ideas in the chapters. Mary and the students talked about what some key concepts were, including that migrant workers work extremely hard for low wages, that migrant workers experience prejudice, and that schooling can provide a way out of poverty. Once key ideas were identified, students again worked in pairs. They listed the key ideas on a piece of butcher paper and located supporting evidence from the texts for these ideas. They cut the examples out of the photocopied pages and pasted them next to the ideas. Then each group shared their examples. This activity helped students understand how to go through a text to find key ideas and then find supporting evidence. Students also worked in groups. Each group summarized one chapter from the book and then shared their summaries. Class discussion helped the students see whether the information they included was important to the summary or not. All of these activities provided important background for the autobiographical essay students would be writing later in the year.

Mary's goal is for all her students to become proficient readers and writers of English. In order to accomplish this goal, she involves students in activities to build their academic language. Mary knows that her students do not use academic language in their everyday conversations, but in order to succeed in school they need to be able to use terms such as *tone*, *voice*, *problem*, *solution*, and *textual evidence*, and they need to be able to employ these concepts in their writing. Mary's lessons scaffolded for her students the development of academic vocabulary and guided her students toward the academic writing they needed to do.

Content knowledge and academic language are keys to the academic success of all students. The teachers we have described in the different scenarios in this book have all helped their students build academic competence by teaching language through content, organizing curriculum around themes, drawing on students' languages and cultures, and emphasizing meaningful reading and writing. In this chapter, we explain academic language in more detail, and we suggest ways that teachers can help students develop academic language.

The importance of developing the language needed for school achievement cannot be underestimated. Marzano (2004), using data from the 2003 U.S. Census Bureau, reports that students who do not graduate from high school have an average yearly income of $10,838, barely above the official poverty level of $9,359. On the other hand, students who graduate from high school have an average yearly income of $18,571, and those who complete college make $35,594 each year. These numbers highlight the importance of helping all students achieve academically.

Academic Language and Conversational Language

One of the first researchers to define academic language was Cummins (2000), who distinguished between basic interpersonal communicative skills (BICS) and cognitive academic language proficiency (CALP). Cummins noted that English language learners were overrepresented in the special education population of schools in Canada. As he investigated reasons for the high number of ELLs who were placed in special education classes, he discovered that although these students appeared to have developed the ability to use English for daily communication, they had difficulty understanding lectures in school, reading textbooks, and writing school papers. In other words, these students spoke and comprehended everyday conversational English quite well, but they lacked the English needed to complete school tasks.

The students were placed in special education classes because many of the tests used to measure English language proficiency tapped only their conversational ability. Since the students did poorly on written tests that measured academic knowledge and problem-solving ability, it was assumed that their scores reflected a cognitive deficit, so they were placed in special education classes. Cummins showed that the low scores actually reflected a lack of academic English, not cognitive deficiencies.

Cummins distinguished between BICS and CALP by considering two dimensions of language: contextual support and cognitive demand. Figure 6.1 represents these two dimensions.

Figure 6.1: **Cummins' Quadrants: Academic and Conversational Language**

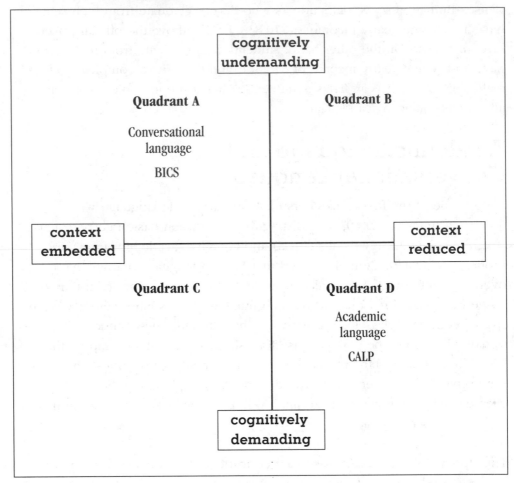

The horizontal axis represents contextual support. It extends from *context-reduced* to *context-embedded*. All language occurs in some context. However, the amount of nonlinguistic support can vary greatly. For example, in talking with someone face to face, we pick up much of the message from tone of voice, facial expression, gestures, and so on. If the conversation is about something we know well, our background knowledge supplies extra context. In addition, if we can see what we are discussing or if we have pictures or other visual cues, it is easier to follow the conversation, even if we lack full language proficiency. A good example of context-embedded language would be discussion about the weather with a friend as we stand in the rain under our umbrellas waiting for a ride to school. Even if some of the words or sentences are not clear, we can follow the thread of the conversation quite well and also contribute to it.

At the other end of the horizontal axis is language that is context-reduced. Here, we have to depend much more on the words than on any other cues. An example might be reading a test question on a standardized test. Often test questions are not related to one another, so other sections of the test do not provide extra clues. In addition, there are no visual cues. The test taker has to rely on knowledge of the language. However, students who take many tests in English build background knowledge of how tests are constructed and worded, along with strategies for answering test questions. This experience, then, builds an internal context about testing and the language of tests that students can draw upon. Without this background knowledge, many ELLs struggle with tests because doing well depends almost entirely on understanding the language with few context clues.

Context-reduced language is not limited to written language. Many ELLs have trouble following lectures in school if the teacher simply talks. On the other hand, the teacher can make the lecture more context-embedded by using a PowerPoint presentation, a graphic organizer, or a video clip. While these supports are helpful for all students, they are especially beneficial for ELLs because the visuals reduce the students' dependency on language for making sense of the lecture.

The vertical scale on Cummins' diagram goes from cognitively undemanding to cognitively demanding. Cognitive demand does not depend so much on the subject as on a person's background knowledge. The conversation about the weather is cognitively undemanding for most people because they know a great deal about weather. They don't need to expend a great deal of mental energy to decide whether it is raining or not. On the other hand, learning a new math concept could be very demanding. A young child learning how to multiply two numbers would have to devote a great deal of attention and memory to the task. Of course, most older students would find multiplication quite easy and not very demanding cognitively.

An example of how cognitive demand changes with experience is driving a car. Someone learning to drive a car may be overwhelmed by all there is to attend to and remember. Which pedal do I push? Which lever do I pull to turn on the windshield wipers? When do I begin to turn the steering wheel? Where do I look if I want to change lanes? For a new driver, driving a car is cognitively demanding. But after a while, driving becomes much easier. I can drive home in the evening after class, and it is almost as though I am on autopilot. My mind is freed up to think about many things other than my driving. I can review how class went or decide what I should do when I get home. And I can do all this while performing the basic driving functions. Driving is not at all cognitively demanding for an experienced driver.

What Cummins found was that many ELLs who were placed in special education classes had a level of English proficiency that allowed them to communicate well orally or in writing when the language was context-embedded and the task was not cognitively demanding. On Figure 6.1 this is the area labeled "Quadrant A." ELLs who function well with context-embedded, cognitively undemanding language have developed BICS, or conversational English proficiency. Studies have shown that it takes about two years for students to develop levels of BICS that are equivalent to those of native English speakers (Collier, 1989). Some students develop conversational proficiency even more quickly. Older ELLs may still pronounce some words with an accent, but they have no difficulty understanding or producing English when there is contextual support and the topic is not too demanding cognitively.

However, an ELL may have developed BICS but still lack CALP. The same student who does well in settings in which English is context-embedded and cognitively undemanding may struggle listening to a lecture or taking a test because in those settings the language is context-reduced and cognitively demanding. Academic language takes from four to nine years to develop (Collier, 1989). That is, an ELL will take several years to score on a par with native English speakers on a standardized test of reading in English. This discrepancy between the time it takes to develop conversational English and the time it takes to develop academic English helps account for the low academic performance of many ELLs who appear to understand and speak English quite well.

Even though the goal of instruction is to help students develop academic language, teaching should not be targeted to quadrant D, where language is cognitively demanding and context-reduced. When administrators ask teachers to prepare students for standardized tests by giving them practice tests frequently or by reading passages similar to those on the test and answering questions, the teaching falls into quadrant D. What ELLs need is instruction that is cognitively demanding but also context-embedded. They need scaffolded instruction to make difficult academic concepts comprehensible. When teachers use graphic organizers, have students work in cooperative groups, and engage them in hands-on activities, they are teaching in quadrant C. They are providing the context while still maintaining high cognitive demand. When teaching occurs in quadrant C, students develop the academic language they need to perform well on tasks that are cognitively demanding and context-reduced.

Cummins' distinction between conversational English and academic English builds on the work of earlier researchers. Cummins (2000) reviews this research. For example, the Russian psychologist Vygotsky distinguished between spontaneous concepts and scientific concepts. Spontaneous concepts, like *brother*, are acquired naturally in the process of growing up with siblings. Scientific concepts, like *brotherhood*, are usually learned in schools. These are more abstract concepts that would not be acquired through everyday experiences. In Cummins' terms, spontaneous concepts are cognitively undemanding, while scientific concepts, at least at first, are cognitively demanding.

What seems clear from this research is that we develop two different kinds of language proficiency. We develop the language we need for social purposes and the language we need for school. Linguists would label these as two different registers of language. A register is made up of certain vocabulary, sentence structures, and text organization. Quite simply, we speak and write differently when we are talking to a school administrator such as the superintendent than when we are talking to our friends at a coffee shop. Even our pronunciation becomes more casual in the coffee-shop setting. Proficient language users can adjust the register they use to fit the setting. What many ELLs lack is the ability to use the academic English register.

In Chapter 1 we distinguished among three types of ELLs: students with adequate formal schooling, those with limited formal schooling, and long-term English learners. Each of these types of students has developed different kinds of language proficiency. Figure 6.2 shows these differences.

Figure 6.2: **Language Proficiency of Three Types of ELLs**

	Language Proficiency			
	conversational language		**academic language**	
	English	L 1	English	L 1
Newly arrived with adequate schooling	(●)	●		●
Newly arrived with limited formal schooling		●		
Long-term English learners	●	●		

As Figure 6.2 indicates, students who come with adequate formal schooling have both conversational and academic proficiency in their first language (L 1). Some students may have also studied some English and may have at least a beginning level of conversational English as indicated by the parentheses on Figure 6.2. These students can read and write at grade level in their first language, and they are also on grade level in the different content areas. Although they need to develop both conversational and academic English, they have a strong base to start from. Cummins' (1981) research shows that knowledge and skills gained in one language transfer to a second language. Students with adequate formal schooling do well in school in English because they can transfer their previous learning. Academic language proficiency in one language is the basis for the development of academic proficiency in a second language.

Students with limited formal schooling, in contrast, lack academic proficiency in their first language. While they have conversational proficiency, they do not have the academic knowledge and skills to transfer from their first language into English. For this reason, these students struggle in school. They are trying to learn both academic subject-matter knowledge and English at the same time.

Long-term English learners often have conversational proficiency in both their first language and English. However, they lack the language needed for school. They do not read and write on grade level in their first language or in English, and, as a result, they are behind in different school subjects. These students would benefit from further development of their first language. But in most cases, first-language instruction is not available for older students, so teachers must make a special effort to help long-term English learners develop academic English.

Other researchers have extended and refined the concept of academic language. For example, Scarcella (2003) describes different dimensions of academic English. One of these, the linguistic dimension, includes the ability to understand oral English that contains academic language and to be able to speak using academic terms. Students need to be able to understand lectures in the different content areas. When teachers use advanced or technical vocabulary such as *anemone* or *epitome*, students need to be able to recognize those terms. They also need to be able to use this vocabulary in class discussions and oral reports.

Students also need to develop academic vocabulary to read and write papers in the different subject areas. Academic vocabulary consists of three kinds of words. The first is *general academic vocabulary*. These are words like *analyze* or *data* that occur in many different content area texts. A second group consists of *content-specific vocabulary*, such as *hypotenuse*, *nucleus*, and *foreshadowing*, that occur most often in one specific content area. A third type of academic vocabulary includes *signal words* like *because* or *finally*. These are words that show relationships among ideas in a text. *Because* signals a cause-effect relationship, while *finally* indicates a sequence.

ELLs need to develop a vocabulary that includes all three types of words. Much of academic vocabulary is acquired through extensive reading of academic texts and by listening to academic lectures. However, some content-specific vocabulary should be taught intentionally to help students grasp key concepts. Later, we suggest ideas for teaching content-specific academic vocabulary directly.

Academic language extends beyond the word level. Sentences in academic writing are different from those in everyday writing and speech. Generally, sentences in academic writing and speech are longer and more complex. Complex sentences carry more information by embedding ideas into dependent clauses. Consider the following sentence that might be found in a social studies text:

> "The colonists who settled on the western banks attempted to grow crops; however, the planting season had passed and the weather in that region had grown cold, so the crops did not sprout as the colonists had expected they would."

This sentence combines six clauses, each conveying a different idea:

- The colonists attempted to grow crops.
- The colonists settled on the western banks.
- The planting season had passed.
- The weather in that region had grown cold.
- The crops did not sprout.
- The colonists had expected the crops would sprout.

Not all these ideas are equally important. There are two main ideas: "The colonists attempted to grow crops" and "The crops did not sprout." The other clauses explain which colonists are being referred to and why the crops did not sprout. The challenge for a second language learner is deciding how the ideas are related and which one or ones are the most important.

The best way for students to develop the ability to comprehend sentences such as these is through engagement with academic texts. If students read extensively in different content areas, they acquire both the academic vocabulary and the academic sentence structure. In addition to extensive reading, ELLs benefit from some specific instruction on the sentence structure of academic texts. One good activity is a sentence-combining exercise. Students take a series of simple sentences and combine them into a more complex sentence.

Students also need to learn how to organize sentences into different kinds of writing demanded by the different subject areas. The autobiographies Mary's students wrote have a different form than a science report or a social studies paper. The different kinds of writing in each content area are referred to as genres. ELLs need to become competent in using a range of genres.

Schleppergrell (2004) has identified different genres used in science and history. In science, for example, students might write a procedure paper. This would be a paper that lists the steps in an experiment. It is a series of instructions. A procedural recount is slightly different. Instead of listing steps that someone should take, it retells what was done during an experimental procedure. One difference between these genres would be the verb forms. A procedure would consist of a series of commands: "Pour the liquid into the container." A procedural recount, on the other hand, would contain past-tense verbs, usually with passive voice to maintain a formal style: "The liquid was poured into the container." In both procedures and procedural recounts, the writer would use signal words such as *first* or *next* as transitions.

Other genres in science include reports and explanations. Reports present information by dividing it into parts or listing its properties. Explanations describe how and why phenomena occur. Each of these genres takes on a certain form. ELLs can become proficient in reading and writing in different genres if teachers carefully scaffold instruction, providing models of good writing and helping students understand exactly how to produce each genre, much the way Mary did for her students.

All students need to develop academic language to succeed in school. This is an especially difficult task for ELLs, and it takes time for them to develop academic language to the same level as their native English-speaking classmates. However, with teacher support they can develop academic English. In the next sections, we suggest some ways to help ELLs develop academic English.

How Can Teachers Help?

ELLs can best develop academic language when teachers organize curriculum around themes and teach language through content. To teach language through content effectively, teachers should develop both content and language objectives and assess each. In addition, teachers can engage students in extensive reading to develop vocabulary and also teach some key vocabulary directly.

Content and Language Objectives

Content objectives specify the knowledge and skills students are to develop in each content area. Generally, these objectives are taken from the state standards. Language objectives can be derived from the content area subject matter. These objectives specify the language forms and functions a student should demonstrate in writing and speaking about content area topics. The TESOL organization (Teachers of English to Speakers of Other Languages) (http://www.TESOL.org) has developed language proficiency standards for listening, speaking, reading, and writing for ELLs at different proficiency levels. This document can be a useful guide for developing language objectives.

Language objectives can be at the text level, the sentence level, or the word level. For example, if the theme is cycles and the students are studying the water cycle, a content objective might be for students to demonstrate their understanding of the water cycle by drawing a diagram and labeling each phase. A text-level language objective could be for students to refer to the diagram and write a science report about the water cycle. At the sentence level, an objective could be for students to use passive voice in their report. And at the word level, the objective could be to use content-specific academic vocabulary such as *precipitation* and *evaporation*. Teachers would not want to assign all the language objectives at one time, but through various assignments they could teach and assess ELLs' developing language proficiency.

To take a second example, if students were studying westward migration in the United States, the content objective might be for students to demonstrate their understanding of the reasons for the westward migration by listing them. A language objective at the text level would be for students to write a historical account. Accounts explain why certain historical events occurred. A language objective at the sentence level might be to use third person in the account to achieve an objective tone. At the word level, students could use general academic vocabulary such as *area* or *migration* in their writing.

When teachers consciously teach both language and content, ELLs benefit. It is important for all teachers who have ELLs in their classes to recognize the importance of teaching not only the academic content but also the language that is appropriate for that content area. Teachers can also assess students in both their content knowledge and their academic language development.

Developing Academic Vocabulary

One important step in helping students develop academic language is teaching the vocabulary of the different content areas. When teachers teach language through content, they teach both the content and the language, so teaching vocabulary involves teaching the concepts that words stand for. For example, a student could be asked to look up the word *triangle* in a dictionary and write a definition. The student could write a sentence using *triangle*. The teacher could even give a quiz on the words students were assigned to look up and write sentences for. However, the students would have only a definition, which would soon be forgotten. This approach to teaching language items without teaching content does not produce the desired result. Unless teachers help students develop the academic concepts that the words represent, the students will only have some useless labels.

On the other hand, when teachers teach language through content, they can engage students in meaningful activities to build concepts and language. For example, a teacher could convey the concept of a triangle through many activities. Students could be involved in hands-on activities at math centers. They could compare triangles with other geometric shapes. They could learn about different kinds of triangles and the properties of triangles. In the process of learning about triangles, students would learn a number of related words, such as *base*, *altitude*, and *hypotenuse*.

It is important for teachers to be sure that students build both the academic content knowledge of the subject areas and the corresponding vocabulary. Marzano (2004) presents research showing the importance of building academic vocabulary. As Marzano states, "Clearly, vocabulary knowledge has a strong, documented relationship with a variety of factors that have been shown to be related to background knowledge, family income or SES, academic achievement, and intelligence" (p. 32).

Marzano reports studies showing that academic achievement is correlated to background knowledge. He cites eight studies that looked at the relationship between background knowledge and academic achievement. The average correlation for these studies is .66. As Marzano explains, a .66 correlation means that a student who gains one standard deviation (from the 50th percentile to the 84th percentile) in academic background knowledge would jump from the 50th percentile to the 75th percentile in academic achievement. For ELLs, building background knowledge is a key to academic success.

One way to build background knowledge is through direct experiences. A teacher can take students to a museum or to a science lab at a local university. While some students are afforded many experiences to build background outside of school, most ELLs do not have these opportunities. Teachers may arrange some field trips, but at most schools, funds are limited. For that reason, most background building is indirect. Three sources for building background indirectly are through educational television, oral language interactions, and reading. All three types of indirect experiences build background knowledge, and they build vocabulary. In addition to showing educational films and video clips, including clips downloaded from the Internet, and engaging students in extended classroom discussion of academic topics, teachers can build students' background knowledge by teaching vocabulary both indirectly through extensive reading and directly through focused vocabulary instruction related to specific content areas.

Extensive Reading

One way to build background knowledge and to raise the academic achievement of ELLs is to provide time for them to read and then talk and write about what they have read. Studies have shown that students acquire vocabulary through extensive reading. Even though all students can increase their vocabulary through wide reading, the number of words they will acquire by seeing them in context varies, depending on the students' reading ability, the grade level, and the density of the text. Better readers and students in higher grades have a greater chance of acquiring new words from context. In addition, students acquire more new words when most of the words in a text are familiar. If the text is too dense (too many unknown words), which is often the case for ELLs, they do not receive enough context clues to acquire many new words.

For that reason, it is important for teachers to develop a reading program that provides all students books at an appropriate level. For teachers of older ELLs, this may mean bringing in magazines and books often used at lower grades. In addition, teachers may want to arrange for students to read with a partner or cross-age reading buddy. Samway (1995) has documented the benefits to ELLs of a cross-age reading buddy program for second language readers. Further, teachers may want to supply some books on tape and CDs so that ELLs can listen to a proficient reader on headsets as they follow along in the text.

Krashen (2004) has summarized the research on what he terms *free voluntary reading* (FVR). Almost without fail, studies have shown that students make gains in reading comprehension when they are given time to read. The few studies that do not show gains were usually very short-term studies. It takes time to establish a routine for independent reading. Students need to learn how to make good choices of books. When teachers give students time to read on a regular basis over the course of at least a semester, the students show clear gains in their reading comprehension.

Although independent reading is an essential component of an effective reading program, it works only if it is implemented correctly. Pilgreen (2000) lists eight key elements of a good *Sustained Silent Reading* (SSR) program for second language learners. First, students need access to appropriate books. Nothing can sink an SSR program more quickly than a lack of books. If students don't find something interesting to read, they won't get hooked on books. Instead, they will interrupt other students who are trying to read. Along the same lines, the books must be appealing. Teachers have found different ways to display books and magazines so that they attract students. For example, they may line them up on the chalkboard or use book racks to display them so that the covers are easily visible. When teachers read books to students, students want to read those same books or other books by the same author on their own. Organizing books by topic can help students find books of interest. Teachers can also include as many books as possible on the current theme they are teaching.

Besides access and appeal, Pilgreen lists a conducive environment as one of the factors that characterizes successful programs. At the very least, the room should be quiet (or relatively quiet, with students reading in pairs) during

SSR. Students should know not to interrupt other readers. Teachers also create conducive environments by bringing in a couch or beanbag chairs for students to sit in as they read. One teacher even created a reading loft. Her students could climb up a ladder to the loft and read their books. Pilgreen also points out that teachers should encourage students to read. Struggling readers often need encouragement. Even when the teacher provides books a struggling reader can read, the student's past experiences might make him or her reluctant to try reading, and for such students an extra nudge may be needed.

In many districts, whole schools have adopted SSR programs. In some cases the programs have failed because the teachers were simply told to plan some time each day for SSR, but they were not given any training in how to develop a good program. Staff training is a key factor in creating effective programs. It helps for all teachers to follow similar procedures. Of course, teachers all need the right books and time in the schedule for SSR.

One factor that Pilgreen lists surprises many people: nonaccountability. By this, she means that students should not be tested or made to write a book report on every book they read. If students have to take a quiz every time they finish a story, SSR quickly loses its appeal. In fact, we have seen schools that have adopted programs that provide books but also provide computerized systems with quizzes and a way to compile student points. In these schools, a class might win a pizza party if the students earn enough points by reading books and passing tests. The problem is that students stop reading for pleasure or information. Instead, they read to pass a quiz. Good readers choose easy books that they can read quickly to pile up points. Although these programs are attractive because they provide books and a computerized management system, they are actually dangerous. Students who are rewarded with points or prizes for reading may not read without those external rewards. The programs can subvert the development of a love of reading.

Even though Pilgreen says that students should not be held accountable for each book they read, she also states that teachers should engage students in different kinds of follow-up activities. She lists a number of these. Students can give oral reports on books or make a poster for a book they liked. They can write a blurb to advertise a book or record an ad for the book. They can create a diorama to represent key ideas in a book. Students who have read the same book can develop a class presentation on the book. Teachers can hold a short conference with a student who has finished a book to talk about what the student learned or what the student liked or disliked about the book.

One teacher we know created a database program where his fifth graders could log in, read other students' comments on a book, and then add their own. Students enjoyed giving their opinion on the books they read and, in the process, they provided evidence that they had read and understood the book. The follow-up activity could also reflect the content of two or three related books. For example, students could create a Venn diagram showing how the books or some of the characters are alike and different. After reading a book, people like to talk about it or share what they have learned, and effective teachers provide students with various ways to do that.

Finally, Pilgreen points out that a good SSR program must provide students with distributed time to read. Just reading for an hour on Friday isn't enough. By the next week, students will have forgotten what they were reading. Instead, students need a set period of time each day or every other day for reading. When students know the schedule for SSR, they begin to look forward to that time, and they make better use of the SSR period. The eight factors Pilgreen lists—access, appeal, conducive environment, encouragement, staff training, nonaccountability, follow-up activities, and distributed time to read—are all important in establishing a good independent reading period.

Direct Vocabulary Instruction

Extensive reading helps students build academic vocabulary. However, in order for ELLs to develop the academic vocabulary and the background knowledge they need for academic achievement, they need direct vocabulary instruction in addition to extensive reading. Direct instruction is effective if teachers choose the right words to teach and teach them in ways supported by research. For example, taking 10 or 20 words a week that "look hard" from a novel or a social studies book, having students look up the words in the dictionary and write a definition, and then giving a vocabulary quiz on Friday is not very effective. Words must be carefully chosen and taught in such a way that all students learn them at a deep level and can use them as they listen, speak, read, and write.

Stahl and Fairbanks (1986) conducted a meta-analysis of studies of direct vocabulary instruction. They found that traditional approaches to teaching vocabulary had only limited utility. On average, studies of traditional vocabulary teaching had an effect size of only .32. In contrast, studies of direct vocabulary instruction targeted to words related to content had a large effect size of .97. This meta-analysis shows that direct instruction works if teachers choose the right words and teach them using the right methods.

Choosing Vocabulary to Teach

Students need to develop the academic vocabulary of the different content areas. Researchers have developed different approaches to categorizing the words that make up academic vocabulary. For example, Beck, McKeown, and Kucan (2002) distinguish among three types of words. Tier 1 words are those, like *dog*, that ELLs probably would know in their first language but lack the label for in English. Tier 1 also includes words that are easy to demonstrate or act out along with common idiomatic expressions. For the most part, Tier 1 words fall more into the conversational language category than the academic language category by Cummins' definition. Teachers don't need to spend much time teaching Tier 1 words since ELLs will pick up many of these outside class.

Tier 2 words, according to Beck and colleagues, are more abstract words than Tier 1 words. An example might be *triangle* or *setting*. In addition, Tier 2 includes words that show connection, like *since*. Tier 2 words form part of the academic vocabulary and require some attention from teachers since many ELLs are not familiar with them. However, Tier 2 also includes cognates. Nearly 80 percent of the ELLs in U.S. schools are Spanish speakers, and estimates of the number of Spanish cognates for English words are as high as 40 percent. So, as we suggested in an earlier chapter, teachers should help students access these cognates.

Tier 3 words are low-frequency words. They usually appear only in content books at the upper grades. Generally, these words are not cognates or at least not cognates of words students are familiar with, and they are difficult to demonstrate. An example of a Tier 3 word might be *algorithm*. Beck and colleagues suggest that teachers focus on teaching the Tier 2 words rather than those in Tiers 1 or 3.

Earlier, we discussed another way of categorizing academic vocabulary: by distinguishing between content-specific vocabulary and general academic vocabulary. Donley and Reppen (2001) define content-specific words as words that are used primarily in one content area. For example, *triangle* is found most often in math, and *mitosis* occurs in biology. General academic vocabulary consists of words not often used in conversational language but used frequently across the academic disciplines. Examples of general academic words would be *hypothesis*, *data*, and *empirical*.

Donley and Reppen point out that context-specific vocabulary is more salient than general academic vocabulary for a number of reasons. These terms are important to the content area, so they are emphasized by teachers. They are also relatively easy to define, partly because they can be compared and contrasted with other words in the discipline. A word like *triangle* can be explained to young students by comparing and contrasting triangles with other geometric shapes. In addition, content-specific vocabulary is often listed in boldface type in textbooks. Frequently, these words appear in a glossary, or they are defined in the text. Even though they don't appear as frequently as general academic vocabulary, students often learn content-specific vocabulary more easily because it is emphasized by teachers and highlighted in texts.

Various lists of general academic vocabulary have been developed. For example, Carroll, Davies, and Richman (1971) compiled *The American Heritage Word Frequency Book* based on 5 million words found in school texts used in grades three though nine. Coxhead (2000) created The Academic Word List based on words in academic texts used at the university level. Although word-frequency lists appear to be useful sources for words to teach, Marzano (2004) points out that computer counts of words result in lists that are quite uneven. Most students would know some of the words. Other words are quite rare and would not be too useful. Marzano gives examples from Harris and Jacobson's list, *Basic Elementary Reading Vocabularies* (Harris & Jacobson, 1972). The sixth-grade list contains both relatively easy words such as *athlete*, *catsup*, *pill*, and *seventeen* along with rare words like *bluster*, *ebb*, *gantry*, and *seethe*. Because these word lists are based on frequency of occurrence, the results often don't match up well with common-sense notions about which words students need to learn.

Marzano offers a different approach to choosing words to teach. Rather than using word lists based on frequency counts, he has looked carefully at national standards in the different subject areas. These standards represent the knowledge and skills that subject-area specialists have determined are crucial for students to know at the different grade levels. Using the standards documents, Marzano and other researchers at the Mid-continent Research for Education and Learning Center have developed two documents. The first is *Content Knowledge: A Compendium of Standards and Benchmarks for K–12 Education* (Kendall & Marzano, 2000). This document "synthesizes more than 100 national and state documents and organizes their content into 14 major categories: mathematics, science, history, English language arts, geography, the arts, civics, economics, foreign language, health, physical education, behavioral studies, technology, and life skills" (p. 111). The second document, *Standards for Excellence* (Marzano, 1998), synthesizes 22 state and national documents organized into eight categories.

Marzano analyzed these documents to determine key vocabulary items that occur consistently in the different content areas at various grade-level clusters. The result is a list of nearly 8,000 terms across 11 subject areas. Terms within each subject area are divided into four levels: K–2, 3–5, 6–8, and 9–12. Clearly, it is not reasonable to assume that during a K–12 span, teachers would teach 8,000 words. Marzano suggests that the total can be reduced to a manageable number by paring the list in various ways. For example, a school might choose just a few subject areas to concentrate on rather than attempting to cover all the areas. A school could also divide the lists into essential and supplementary words.

Once the number of words has been reduced, schools could decide how many words per week should be taught at different grade levels. Marzano suggests a schedule that begins with just one word each week in first grade and increases gradually. By tenth grade, students would be responsible for 25 words per week. Following this plan, more than 4,000 words could be taught during the K–12 years. This seems like a reasonable target. The advantage of Marzano's plan is that the words being taught are those essential to each content area. Knowledge of these words would increase students' background knowledge and their academic achievement.

A Method for Direct Vocabulary Instruction

A number of researchers have developed methods for teaching vocabulary directly. Newer methods avoid the traditional approach of having students look up the words, write them in sentences, and then take a test, an approach that has not resulted in significant gains in vocabulary knowledge. Graves reviews several current methods in *The Vocabulary Book* (2006). These methods generally involve engaging the students in more detailed activities to learn and use vocabulary the teacher has chosen.

Marzano (2004) has developed a method of teaching vocabulary based on research evidence. This method incorporates elements found to be effective in helping students develop a deep understanding of key terms. Marzano's approach involves six steps:

1. The teacher provides a description, explanation, or example of the new term. Here the teacher might tell a story using the term or bring in pictures to exemplify the term.
2. The students are asked to restate the description, explanation, or example in their own words. Students might also write their response in their vocabulary notebook.
3. For this step, students draw a picture or create a graphic to represent the term. Research has shown that using both linguistic and nonlinguistic information helps store items in long-term memory. This step is especially helpful for ELLs.
4. The teacher engages students in activities that help them discuss and review the terms they have written in their notebooks. For example, students might compare and contrast terms or create metaphors using the terms.
5. At specific points, students are asked to look back at their vocabulary notebooks and refine the descriptions or explanations of the terms they have listed. They could also work in groups to discuss the terms and explain the terms to one another.
6. The final step is to involve students in word games using the key terms.

Rather than studying a few words each week and then forgetting them, students in classes using Marzano's methods look at and think about key terms repeatedly. Over time, students' understanding of the words in their notebooks deepens, and students retain this knowledge. Direct vocabulary study of words taken from different content areas along with a program of extensive reading that includes different genres important to the various content areas can increase ELLs' vocabulary and background knowledge and can raise their levels of academic achievement. A final scenario shows how one teacher helps her students build academic language.

Where We Live Influences How We Live: Building Academic Language

Jill teaches world studies at a small, rural high school. She plans her lessons to meet state standards that ask students to understand how physical, economic, and social processes shape cultural patterns and characteristics in various places and regions. In addition, students must come to understand how people, places, and environments are connected and interdependent. Jill realizes these are complex ideas and that her social studies text is not always organized or written in ways that students easily understand.

In one of her classes, she has five ELLs, and in another she has two. All are at a low intermediate level of English proficiency, and several of them have limited formal schooling. Jill knows that these students struggle to read the text and make sense of her course and that several of her native English speakers struggle to read the social studies text as well. Jill decides to use Freire's *Problem Posing* approach (Wallerstein, 1987) to teach a unit that she hopes will help all her students develop important concepts and the academic language related to social studies. Standards require that students use problem solving as they study, so this approach fits nicely into her planning. She also plans specific activities that will make the social studies concepts more comprehensible to her ELLs and to her struggling readers.

Freire developed Problem Posing as a way to help older students learn a second language and also develop the language they needed to improve their lives. Problem Posing involves six steps:

1. Begin with the learners' actual experiences. Draw on the students' background knowledge.

2. Develop background concepts through actions, visual aids, and discussion.

3. Begin critical observation using pictures, books, personal stories and experiences, and community events.

4. Through comparison and contrast help students view concept(s) and understand how those concepts relate to their lives.

5. Research the concepts through reading, writing, interviews, discussions, films, and field trips.

6. Plan appropriate action(s) related to students' own lives and resulting in social change.

Jill feels that this approach offers the structure her students need because the social studies concepts can be related to the students' own lives and interests. She plans carefully to help students gain both the key concepts and the academic language needed to talk, read, and write about social studies. As she plans the unit of study, Jill writes content and language objectives for each of her lessons.

The first activities, based on the first two steps of the Problem Posing model, are designed to help students develop the important social studies concept of a community as a group of people who are interdependent or interactive in some way, presumably to serve some purposes. During the first two steps of Problem Posing, teachers begin with students' experiences and then build important concepts. Jill begins the unit by discussing the idea that individuals are part of different communities. She draws three columns on the board. Over the first column she writes "close friends." Then she does a think-aloud to model who some of her friends are, and she writes their names on the board. She repeats this procedure to list neighbors and to list people she spends time with at the school. Then she asks students to make their own lists for each category.

After students have completed their lists, Jill draws three overlapping circles on the board and puts the names from her lists in the circles. She puts some names in the overlap between two of the circles. Some fit in all three. Then she directs her students to make their own Venn diagrams to represent the communities they are part of. When students complete their diagrams, she has them share the results in small groups. She notices that her ELLs can participate quite well using the diagrams to support their talk. She plans to come back to this structure later in the unit and have students brainstorm and categorize the different roles community members take as they work, study, worship, engage in politics, and participate in recreational activities.

Once her students begin to develop the concept of community in general, Jill wants them to examine their particular community more closely. She has students work in teams to interview various people around the school: the principal, the bus driver, the cafeteria workers, and the nurse. Once groups collect the interview information, Jill involves them in a jigsaw activity. She forms new groups with one or more members of each interview team. The new groups each write a report on the roles and responsibilities of the members of their school community. Once the groups write their reports, the class creates a composite paper using information from all of the groups. Jill is pleased to see that the ELLs in her class participated actively in the interviews and the group activities. These activities allow Jill to introduce academic terms from social studies, such as *role* and *interdependence*.

Jill feels that these initial activities have helped her students understand the concept of community as a group of interdependent people who play different roles. Now Jill wants her students to start to focus on how the environment influences community life. Following steps three and four of the Problem Posing model, Jill engages her students in activities that foster critical observation and problem solving. She wants them to further develop key concepts by comparing and contrasting communities. Jill's students have spent time building the concept of community by examining the communities they are a part of. Now she wants them to analyze communities with which they have not had direct, personal experience.

Jill divides her class into heterogeneous groups of four or five. She gives each group two pictures of different kinds of environments (city, village, ocean, countryside, desert). Each group has a different pair of pictures. Jill asks the students to list characteristics of these areas. She tells them to write down anything that comes to their minds, including descriptive words such as *quiet, noisy, isolated, hot, dry,* and *rainy* or nouns such as *sand, water,* or *buildings*. After the groups have developed lists for each picture, they post their pictures on the board and list their words under the pictures. As a whole class, they discuss the pictures and the words the groups have developed. This activity serves two purposes. For students with limited English proficiency, it provides important vocabulary, which is supported by the use of the pictures. At the same time, all the students begin to think about the physical characteristics of different environments.

As a writing assignment, Jill asks her students to choose two pictures and write an essay, comparing and contrasting the areas shown in the pictures. She begins by choosing a picture of a city area and another of a rural area. She moves these two pictures to another area on the board and under them she draws a Venn diagram. Using the words the students have brainstormed, she fills in the circles. Then she asks for additional words to describe each picture and adds them to the diagram. She also adds some words of her own. This gives her a chance to introduce academic vocabulary important for social studies, such as *densely populated* and *low population density*. Next, she explains how she could use the diagram to help structure her comparison-contrast essay. She also notes that she could use the vocabulary from the diagrams in her essay. She gives students time to choose the pictures they will use for their essays, draw a Venn diagram like hers, and copy words to use in their essays. In subsequent lessons, students write drafts of their essays, confer with classmates and their teacher, revise their essays, edit them, and then submit them to Jill. This writing assignment gives students opportunities to write and talk using key vocabulary needed to describe different areas.

To further develop social studies concepts related to the different environments, Jill asks students to work in their groups once more. She gives each group one of the pictures they described earlier and asks them to list some of the needs of people living in the area. They brainstorm what people would need to (1) survive and (2) live comfortably. As before, groups post their pictures and lists on the board for class discussion. During the discussions, Jill adds more terms to each list.

After the class has discussed all the pictures, Jill asks them to return to their groups and consider for their picture the advantages and disadvantages of living in that place. One group with a picture of busy city streets made the following lists:

Living in the City

Advantages	Disadvantages
easy to shop	crowded
good entertainment	too much crime
live near friends	live alone
more choices of things to do	polluted
easy to get places	noisy

Jill asks students to use the information they have generated in their group to write a short individual paper outlining the pros and cons of living in that area. She suggests a structure for this comparison-contrast paper and then lets the students work individually. Once again, the ELLs and struggling readers in Jill's class benefited from the clear structure, the background knowledge they built during the unit, and the specific vocabulary their group had brainstormed. As a result, many of the students wrote excellent papers.

Jill wants to make these concepts more concrete, so she arranges with a friend of hers who is teaching social studies to advanced English learners in a city in Japan to exchange information about their respective communities. She explains to her class that they are going to e-mail letters to the Japanese students. She asks them to describe their own rural community to their pen pal, using vivid language that would enable the pen pal to recognize their area on a visit.

The students in Japan complete the same assignment describing their area, and the students exchange e-mail letters. Each student then writes a second letter asking for clarification or additional details. These activities help Jill's students examine their own community carefully. Once all the students in each class have a good idea of what life in the other community is like, the students e-mail pictures taken around their community. Then the class discusses how the pictures are similar to and different from what they expected from reading the letters. This activity helps them understand the importance of careful observation and description, important tools for social scientists. Jill knows that pen-pal letter activity provided a further opportunity for her students to develop the vocabulary and grammatical structures they need for social studies.

During step five of Problem Posing, students conduct further research through reading. Jill forms new groups and gives each group a short article about an interesting community. For example, one article tells how people in a crowded city create rooftop gardens. Another article describes the ice sculptures people in a northern Chinese city make each winter. Next, Jill asks each group to complete an activity. She gives them these directions:

1. Appoint a recorder.

2. Look over the article in your groups. Think about the needs of the people who live here. How do they meet these needs? What kinds of homes, jobs, clothes, and so on are important? How is this place different from where you live? What would be the hardest/easiest aspect of living in this place?

3. Pick out characteristics of the place described in the article that affect what people do and how people live in that place.

4. List some of the characteristics and some examples of how the characteristics affect what people do and how they live. Put your results on a chart as shown here.

Characteristics	What People Do
_____	_____
_____	_____
_____	_____

Each group posts their picture and chart on the bulletin boards around the room. Students then have time to walk around the room to examine each picture and chart and record interesting details in their social studies notebooks. They use this information for a class discussion.

After students have discussed what they observed, they work to develop a PowerPoint presentation to show their classmates. They scan in pictures from the article and list key ideas that show how both the natural and the built environments influence how people live. All the students enjoy watching the presentations.

As a follow-up activity, Jill asks each group to find additional information about how the environment influences life in a community like the one they read about. Students look in books and magazines in the library or search on the Internet for additional information. Each student finds a different source of information and brings it to the group to share. Using this information, each group develops a PowerPoint presentation that includes scans of pictures and key ideas from their articles. This activity extends the knowledge Jill's students are building about how the environment influences how people live. As they read articles and books, Jill's students continue to build their academic language.

The final step of Problem Posing involves community research and an action plan. During this step, students put social studies into action. Jill begins this phase of her unit by having her students refocus on their own communities. She lists these questions on the board: How did our community develop the way it did? Why do we have the kinds of homes built here? Why do we wear certain kinds of clothes and buy certain products? How does our community use the resources it has? How does the environment relate to the jobs that adults and children have? Students brainstorm answers to these questions and conduct research to find out information they did not know. One day, they invite older community members to come to the class. Small groups of students interview the seniors to find out more about how the community developed over time.

Once Jill's students have gathered more information about their community, they begin to evaluate the quality of life there. Jill lists the following questions on the board:

Advantages and Disadvantages of Living in Our Community

1. What are some advantages and disadvantages of living in our community?

2. How can we obtain more information about some of the things we have listed as advantages and disadvantages?

3. How do we affect the quality of life in the place we live? Positively? Negatively?

4. How can we improve the quality of life in our community?

After her students have brainstormed the positive and negative aspects of living in their community, they conduct further research to find out more about some of the things they listed. Since they live in a small town, one of the disadvantages is the lack of entertainment for teens. They decide to invite the mayor in and ask her questions about the town's supporting new development, such as building a recreation center. Jill also brings in a copy of the annual budget report so students can better understand how the town spends its funds.

Once students have more information, Jill helps them formulate a plan for social action. The students decide to make a presentation to the city council, requesting that funds be allocated to build and maintain a recreational center for the teenagers in the town. Once they decide on their course of action, the students conduct further research and develop a detailed presentation. They also learn how to get on the council meeting agenda and learn about proper procedures for presentations. By using a Problem Posing approach to social studies, Jill helped all of her students, especially her English language learners, build important concepts and academic language during this unit of study.

Conclusion

All students need to develop academic language to attain high levels of academic achievement. Academic language is the language used in the various academic fields. Each subject has certain ways of organizing and presenting ideas, so students need to learn the different genres used in each area. They also need to become familiar with writing that includes complex sentences and an impersonal, objective style. Perhaps the biggest challenge is for students to develop the vocabulary of the content areas. Teachers can help students develop academic language by writing language objectives for each content objective and then monitoring students' development of both content area knowledge and academic language. As the two scenarios in this chapter show, when teachers focus on helping students develop academic language, all their students, including the English language learners, benefit.

Applications for Chapter 6

1. We discussed Cummins' quadrants and the kinds of language students need to understand and use when the language is context-embedded and when it is context-reduced. Think about four different activities you have done with your students or that you have observed a teacher doing recently. Were those activities context-embedded or context-reduced? Explain what made the activities context-embedded or context-reduced.

2. Review the state standards for your grade level or your content area. Pick out at least five topics from those standards. Will those topics be cognitively demanding or cognitively undemanding for ELLs? Explain why.

3. Figure 6.2 (page 156) shows three types of ELLs and indicates which types of language proficiency each type of learner has. Consider students you have taught or are teaching and determine if they have conversational language, academic language, or both in English.

4. There are basically three kinds of academic vocabulary: general academic vocabulary, content-specific words, and signal words. With a partner, brainstorm at least ten words of each kind to share with the class.

5. What are some of the different genres that students need to recognize and use for your classroom? Explain.

6. Choose one topic from a standard you need to teach. Write a content objective and a language objective for that topic.

7. If you have an SSR program in your school or classroom or have observed SSR in a school, review Pilgreen's key elements for good SSR programs. Which of these elements are in place in your school or the school you observed? Which are missing?

8. Marzano suggests six steps for effective vocabulary teaching. Using his model, teach three words over the next week. Report back on the success of this approach.

9. Explain how Jill or Mary helped their students develop academic language. What specific activities led to the development of academic language?

Glossary

acquisition – The process of "picking up" a language naturally without formal instruction (see **learning**).

acquisition/learning hypothesis – Krashen distinguishes between acquiring a language by receiving messages we understand and learning a language through formal study. He hypothesizes that we develop proficiency in a language through acquisition rather than through learning.

adequate formal schooling student – A recent arrival who enters school on grade level in the content areas and with literacy in the first language.

affective filter hypothesis – Krashen hypothesizes that there is a kind of mental filter that can block comprehensible input from reaching the part of the brain that processes language. Factors that can raise the filter and block input include boredom, nervousness, or lack of motivation.

basic interpersonal communicative skills (BICS) – Cummins defines BICS or *conversational language* as language that is both context-embedded and cognitively undemanding. It takes ELLs about two years to develop BICS.

bilingual education – Any program that makes some use of both a student's primary language and English for instruction.

cognates – Words that come from the same root. These are words that are related across languages, such as *biología* in Spanish and *biology* in English.

Cognitive Academic Language Learning Approach (CALLA) – Developed by Chamot and O'Malley, this content-based approach to language teaching emphasizes the development of metacognition and strategies for learning language through content study.

cognitive academic language proficiency (CALP) – Cummins defines CALP as language that is context-reduced and cognitively demanding. It takes four to nine years for ELLs to develop CALP.

common underlying proficiency (CUP) – Cummins argues that there is a common proficiency that underlies languages. What people learn in one language is also known in the second language.

communicative approach – An approach to teaching ESL that focuses on communication, usually through teaching dialogues or role play. An example is ALM, the Audiolingual Method.

comprehensible input – Krashen's term for messages that a language learner understands. Krashen argues that comprehensible input is necessary for second language acquisition.

concurrent translation – Saying something in one language and then translating it immediately into the second language. This approach to teaching ELLs is not effective.

content objective – A teaching objective taken from an academic content area that specifies either the declarative or procedural knowledge students should develop.

content specific vocabulary – Vocabulary specific to a particular academic content area, such as *rectangle* for geometry.

content-based language teaching – An approach that teaches language through the different content areas rather than focusing on aspects of the language itself.

context-embedded language – Language that is supported by extralinguistic features, such as the physical setting, gestures, tone of voice, etc.

context-reduced language – Language that is not supported by extralinguistic features. An example is a standardized test.

culturally relevant books – Books in which the setting, characters, language, or events correspond to those of its readers.

early exit bilingual program – Also known as *transitional programs*, these bilingual programs use students' first languages as a bridge to English. Students exit the program after about two years or when they develop conversational English.

English as a second language (ESL) – Refers to programs for English language learners in which English is the medium of instruction. ESL instruction may be traditional grammar-based, communicative, or content-based.

English Language Development (ELD) – Content-based programs designed to teach ELLs English. The focus is on English language development rather than on grade-level content instruction. ELD is a term most often used in California.

ESL pull-out program – An ESL program for which ELLs are pulled out of a mainstream classroom for English language instruction, which often focuses on vocabulary or grammar.

free voluntary reading (FVR) – A program during which students are given time to read books of their choice. Generally, they are not tested on the books. Also called Sustained Silent Reading (SSR) or DEAR (Drop Everything and Read).

general academic vocabulary – Vocabulary that is found in many different academic content area texts but not found often in conversational language; for example, *data* or *analysis*.

generative linguistics – Based on Chomsky's theory of language. Generative linguistics attempts to formulate a small set of rules that could generate all and only the grammatical sentences of a language.

input hypothesis – Krashen's hypothesis that language development results from receiving comprehensible input at a level slightly above a person's current level of proficiency.

language acquisition device (LAD) – The term for the area of the brain that processes language input.

language objective – A teaching objective focused on some aspect of language at the word, sentence, or text level.

late exit bilingual program – A bilingual program designed to help students maintain their first language by continuing L1 instruction as well as learn English for five or six years before they exit to all-English instruction.

learning – Krashen's term for aspects of language that are specifically taught and consciously developed. Krashen contrasts learning with acquisition.

limited formal schooling – Students who enter U.S. schools with little to no schooling in their L1. These students must develop both English and subject-area knowledge.

linguistic cue systems – These cueing systems include graphophonics, semantics, and syntax. Good readers use all three effectively and efficiently.

long-term English learner – Students who speak and understand English but struggle with reading and writing in English. These students entered school speaking a language other than English, had limited instruction in their L1, and have spent seven or more years in U.S. schools.

monitor hypothesis – One of Krashen's hypotheses, which holds that L2 learners draw upon their learned knowledge of L2 to monitor their speaking and writing.

Natural Approach – An approach to teaching ESL to elementary students that emphasizes comprehensible input and is organized around topics such as families, plants, and animals.

natural order hypothesis – One of Krashen's hypotheses, which holds that L2 learners acquire certain features of the language, such as the *s* on third-person verbs, in a natural order immune to direct teaching.

newcomers center – A program in which the goal is to help students who have just arrived in the United States adjust to U.S. schooling and learn some basic conversational English and content knowledge.

picture walk – A strategy teachers use with picture books to preview the book by showing the pages of the book and discussing the book before reading it.

preview/view/review – A strategy that helps teachers decide when to use students' first languages to support learning. Content is previewed in a student's first language, then viewed in English through comprehensible input, and reviewed in the first language.

primary language – The first language, heritage language, or native language of any person.

Problem Posing – Freire's six-step approach to language and literacy development that begins with students' experiences and involves critical observation, connecting to students' lives, and ends with students taking action.

psychological strategies – Subconscious strategies, such as predicting or inferring, that readers use naturally to make meaning from texts.

second language students – Students who come to school speaking a language or languages other than English and need support to study in English.

sheltered content instruction – Instruction for ELLs using techniques to make the academic content taught in English more comprehensible. This approach allows students to learn language and content at the same time.

Sheltered Instruction Observation Protocol Model (SIOP) – An approach that employs a checklist to determine whether all the elements of effective instruction for ELLs are present in a sheltered lesson.

signal words – English words like *because* or *finally* that show relationships among ideas in a sentence or text.

small and scattered ELL population – Schools or districts that have only a few ELLs. The ELLs may be spread out across the district.

Specially Designed Academic Instruction in English (SDAIE) – This approach is for ELLs with more advanced levels of English proficiency and at least some background in the subject areas. Teachers make accommodations for students' limited English proficiency as they teach the different academic subjects and test students' knowledge of subject-area content.

Structured English Immersion (SEI) – Instruction for ELLs, usually in a mainstream class. The teacher uses various techniques to make English input comprehensible.

sustained silent reading (SSR) – A period of time provided in classrooms or schools during which students are allowed to read without interruption.

text set – A combination of books organized around a topic that includes books at different difficulty levels.

Total Physical Response (TPR) – An ESL strategy developed by Asher used mainly with beginning ELLs that has students respond to simple commands such as "touch your nose," "open the door," or "point to the blackboard."

Universal Grammar (UG) – A theory of language posited by Chomsky that holds that humans are born with the basic structures of all human languages already present in the brain or an innate knowledge of language.

Professional References

Asher, J. (1977). *Learning another language through actions: The complete teacher's guide*. Los Gatos, CA: Sky Oaks Publications.

Beck, I., McKeown, M., & Kucan, L. (2002). *Bringing words to life: Robust vocabulary instruction*. New York: The Gilford Press.

Berman, P. (1992). *Meeting the challenge of language diversity: An evaluation of programs for pupils with limited proficiency in English*. (Executive Summary No. R-119/1). Berkeley, CA: BW Associates.

Bridgeland, J., Dilulio, J., & Morison, K. B. (2006). *The silent epidemic: Perspectives of high school dropouts*. Washington, DC: Civic Enterprises.

Carroll, J. B., Davies, P., & Richman, B. (1971). *The American heritage word frequency book*. New York: American Heritage Publishing.

Chamot, A., & O'Malley, M. (1989). The cognitive academic language learning approach. In P. Rigg & V. Allen (Eds.), *When they don't all speak English: Integrating the ESL student into the regular classroom* (pp. 108–125). Urbana, IL: NCTE.

Chomsky, N. (1965). *Aspects of the theory of syntax*. Cambridge, MA: M.I.T. Press.

Christian, D. (2000). *Advancing the achievement of English language learners: A research perspective*. Paper presented at the Fourth Annual Claiborne Pell Education Policy Seminar, Brown University, Providence, RI.

Collier, V. (1989). How long? A synthesis of research on academic achievement in a second language. *TESOL Quarterly, 23(3)*, 509–532.

Corson, D. (1995). *Using English words*. New York: Kluwer.

Cortés, C. (1986). The education of language minority students: A contextual interaction model. In D. Holt (Ed.), *Beyond language: Social and cultural factors in schooling language minority students* (pp. 3–33). Los Angeles: Evaluation, Dissemination, and Assessment Center, California State University, Los Angeles.

Coxhead, A. (2000). A new academic word list. *TESOL Quarterly, 34(2)*, 213–238.

Crawford, J. (2004). *Educating English learners*. Los Angeles: Bilingual Education Services.

Cummins, J. (1981). The role of primary language development in promoting educational success for language minority students. In *Schooling and language-minority students: A theoretical framework* (pp. 3–49). Los Angeles: Evaluation, Dissemination and Assessment Center, California State University, Los Angeles.

Cummins, J. (1994). The role of primary language development in promoting educational success for language minority students. In *Schooling and language minority students: A theoretical framework* (pp. 3–46). Los Angeles: Evaluation, Dissemination and Assessment Center, California State University, Los Angeles.

Cummins, J. (2000). *Language, power and pedagogy: Bilingual children in the crossfire*. Tonawanda, NY: Multilingual Matters.

Dooling, D. & Lachman, R. (1971). Effects of comprehension on retention of prose. *Journal of Experimental Psychology, 88(2)*, 216–222.

Donley, K., & Reppen, R. (2001). Using corpus tools to highlight academic vocabulary in SCL T. *TESOL Journal, Autumn*, 7–12.

Dulay, H., & Burt, M. (1974). Natural sequences in child second language acquisition. *Language Learning, 24*, 37–53.

Freeman, D., & Freeman, Y. (1993). Strategies for promoting the primary languages of all students. *The Reading Teacher, 46(7)*, 552–558.

Freeman, D., & Freeman, Y. (2000). *Teaching reading in multilingual classrooms.* Portsmouth, NH: Heinemann.

Freeman, D., & Freeman, Y. (2001). *Between worlds: Access to second language acquisition* (2nd ed.). Portsmouth, NH: Heinemann.

Freeman, D., & Freeman, Y. (2004). *Essential linguistics: What you need to know to teach reading, ESL, spelling, phonics, and grammar.* Portsmouth, NH: Heinemann.

Freeman, Y., Freeman, A., & Freeman, D. (2003). Home run books: Connecting students to culturally relevant texts. *NABE News, 26(3),* 5–8, 11–12.

Freeman, Y., & Freeman, D. (2002). Keys for success for struggling older English learners. *NABE News, 25(3),* 5–7, 37.

Freeman, Y., Freeman, D., & Mercuri, S. (2005). *Dual language essentials for teachers and administrators.* Portsmouth, NH: Heinemann.

Freeman, Y., & Freeman, D. (1991). Ten tips for monolingual teachers of bilingual students. In K. Goodman, L. Bird, & Y. Goodman (Eds.), *The whole language catalog* (p. 90). Santa Rosa, CA: American School Publishers.

Freeman, Y., & Freeman, D. (1998). *ESL/EFL teaching: Principles for success.* Portsmouth, NH: Heinemann.

Freire, P., & Macedo, D. (1987). *Literacy: Reading the word and the world.* South Hadley, MA: Bergin and Garvey.

García, E. (2002). *Student cultural diversity: Understanding and meeting the challenge* (3rd ed.). Boston: Houghton Mifflin.

García, G. (2000). *Lessons from research: What is the length of time it takes limited English proficient students to acquire English and succeed in an all-English classroom?* Washington, DC: National Clearinghouse for Bilingual Education.

Goldenberg, C. (1996). The education of language-minority students: Where are we, and where do we need to go? *The Elementary School Journal, 96(3),* 353–361.

Goodman, K. (1996). *On reading.* Portsmouth, NH: Heinemann.

Goodman, Y. (1982). Retellings of literature and the comprehension process. *Theory into Practice: Children's Literature,* XXI(4), 301–307.

Graves, M. (2006). *The vocabulary book.* New York: Teachers College Press.

Greene, J. (1998). *A meta-analysis of the effectiveness of bilingual education.* Claremont, CA: Tomas Rivera Policy Institute.

Harris, A. J., & Jacobson, M. D. (1972). *Basic elementary reading vocabularies.* London: Collier-Macmillan Limited.

Harrisburg School District. (2006). *Welcome to English as a second language.* From http://www.hbgsd.k12.pa.us/.

Housman, N., & Martinez, M. (2002). *Preventing school dropout and ensuring success for English language learners and Native American students.* Washington, DC: National Clearinghouse for Comprehensive School Reform.

Jiménez, R. (1997). The strategic reading abilities and potential of five low-literacy Latina/o readers in middle school. *Reading Research Quarterly, 32(2),* 224–243.

Kendall, J. S., & Marzano, R. J. (2000). *Content knowledge: A compendium of standards and benchmarks for k–12 education.* Alexandria, VA: Association for Supervision and Curriculum Development.

Krashen, S. (1985). *Inquiries and insights.* Haywood, CA: Alemany Press.

Krashen, S. (1996). *Under attack: The case against bilingual education.* Culver City, CA: Language Education Associates.

Krashen, S. (2003). *Explorations in language acquisition and use.* Portsmouth, NH: Heinemann.

Krashen, S. (2004). *The power of reading: Insights from the research* (2nd ed.). Portsmouth, NH: Heinemann.

Krashen, S., & Terrell, T. (1983). *The Natural Approach: Language acquisition in the classroom.* Hayward, CA: Alemany Press.

Kucer, S., & Silva, C. (2006). *Teaching the dimensions of literacy.* Mahwah, NJ: Lawrence Erlbaum Associates.

Kucer, S., & Tuten, J. (2003). Revisiting and rethinking the reading process. *Language Arts, 80 (4),* 284–290.

Marzano, R. (1998). *Standards for excellence in education.* Washington, DC: Author.

Marzano, R. (2004). *Building background knowledge for academic achievement: Research on what works in schools.* Alexandria, VA: Association for Supervision and Curriculum Development.

Olsen, L., & Jaramillo, A. (1999). *Turning the tides of exclusion: A guide for educators and advocates for immigrant students.* Oakland, CA: California Tomorrow.

Paulson, E. & Freeman, A. (2003). *Insight from the eyes.* Portsmouth, NH: Heinemann.

Pearson, P. D., & Gallagher, M. C. (1983). The instruction of reading comprehension. *Contemporary Educational Psychology, 8(3),* 317–344.

Pilgreen, J. (2000). *The SSR handbook: How to organize and manage a sustained silent reading program.* Portsmouth, NH: Heinemann.

Ramírez, J. D. (1991). *Final report: Longitudinal study of structured English immersion strategy, early-exit and late-exit bilingual education programs* (No. 300-87-0156). Washington, DC: U.S. Department of Education.

Rodríguez, T. A. (2001). From the known to the unknown: Using cognates to teach English to Spanish-speaking literates. *The Reading Teacher, 54(8),* 744–746.

Rolstad, K., Mahoney, K., & Glass, G. (2005). A meta-analysis of program effectiveness research on English language learners. *Educational Policy, 19(4),* 572–594.

Ruíz, R. (1984). Orientations in language planning. *Journal of the National Association of Bilingual Education, 8,* 15–34.

Samway, K., Whang, G., & Pippitt, M. (1995). *Buddy reading: Cross-age tutoring in a multicultural school.* Portsmouth, NH: Heinemann.

Scarcella, R. (2003). *Accelerating academic English: A focus on the English learner.* Irvine, CA: University of California, Irvine.

Schleppergrell, M. J. (2004). *The language of schooling: A functional linguistics perspective.* Mahwah, NJ: Lawrence Erlbaum.

Short, K., Harste, J., & Burke, C. (1996). *Creating classrooms for authors and inquirers.* Portsmouth, NH: Heinemann.

Smith, F. (1985). *Reading without nonsense* (2nd ed.). New York: Teachers College Press.

Saint Paul Public Schools. (2006). English language learner programs. From http://www.ell.spps.org.

Stahl, S. A., & Fairbanks, M. M. (1986). The effects of vocabulary instruction: A model-based meta-analysis. *Review of Educational Research, 56(1),* 72–110.

Wallerstein, N. (1987). Problem posing education: Freire's method for transformation. In I. Shor (Ed.), *Freire for the classroom* (pp. 33–44). Portsmouth, NH: Heinemann.

webmaster@fresno.k12.ca.us. (2006, 2004). Fresno unified school district—facts and figures. Retrieved June 26, 2006, from http://www.fresno.k12.ca.us/.

Wiggins, G., & McTighe, J. (2000). *Understanding by design.* New York: Prentice Hall.

Williams, J. (2001). Classroom conversations: Opportunities to learn for ESL students in mainstream classrooms. *The Reading Teacher, 54(8),* 750–757.

Willig, A. (1985). A meta-analysis of selected studies on the effectiveness of bilingual education. *Review of Educational Research, 55,* 269–317.

www.brookings.edu/metro/pubs/20051012_concentratedpoverty.htm

www.ncela.gwu.edu. (2006). The growing numbers of limited-English-proficient students 1993/94–2003/04. Retrieved June 26, 2006.

Literature References

Ada, A. F. (1990a). *Just one seed*. Carmel, CA: Hampton-Brown.

Ada, A. F. (1990b). *Una semilla nada más*. Carmel, CA: Hampton-Brown.

Ada, A. F. (1991). *Días y días de poesía*. Carmel, CA: Hampton-Brown.

Ada, A. F. (1993). *Canción de todos los niños del mundo*. Boston: Houghton Mifflin Company.

Ada, A. F. (2002). *I love Saturdays y domingos*. New York: Atheneum Books.

Aliki. (1998). *Marianthe's Story: Painted words and spoken memories*. New York: Greenwillow Books.

Almada, P. (1993a). *El mosquito*. Crystal Lake, IL: Rigby.

Almada, P. (1993b). *La mosca*. Crystal Lake, IL: Rigby.

Almada, P. (1997a). *Del padre al hijo*. Crystal Lake, FL: Rigby.

Almada, P. (1997b). *From father to son*. Crystal Lake, IL: Rigby.

Anzaldúa, G. (1993). *Friends from the other side/Amigos del otro lado*. San Francisco: Children's Book Press.

Bacon, R. (1997). *Jessie's flower*. Crystal Lake, IL: Rigby.

Badt, K. (1994). *Good morning, let's eat*. Chicago: Children's Press.

Badt, K. (1995). *Pass the bread*. Chicago: Children's Press.

Baer, E. (1990). *This is the way we go to school: A book about children around the world*. New York: Scholastic.

Bennett, P. (1999). *Under the ocean*. New York: Scholastic.

Berger, M. (1996). *The mighty ocean*. New York: Newbridge Communications Inc.

Bogart, J. E. (1995). Growing. New York: Scholastic.

Boland, J. (1998a). *Girasoles*. Katonah, NY: Richard C. Owen.

Boland, J. (1998b). *Sunflowers*. Katonah, NY: Richard C. Owen.

Bolton, F., & Snowball, D. (1985). *Growing radishes and carrots*. New York: Scholastic.

Bunting, E. (1996). *Sunflower house*. New York: Trumpet.

Bunting, E. (1998). *Going home*. New York: HarperTrophy.

Burke, M. B. (2004). *That's about right: A book about estimating*. Barrington, IL: Rigby.

Canizares, S. (1998). *Butterfly*. New York: Scholastic.

Canizares, S., & Chanko, P. (1998). *What do insects do?* New York: Scholastic.

Canizares, S., & Reid, M. (1993). *Where do insects live?* New York: Scholastic.

Cappellini, M. (1993). *La mariquita*. Crystal Lake, IL: Rigby.

Carden, M., & Cappellini, M. (1997a). *I am of two places*. Crystal Lake, IL: Rigby.

Carden, M., & Cappellini, M. (1997b). *Soy de dos lugares*. Crystal Lake, IL: Rigby.

Carle, E. (1969). *The very hungry caterpillar*. Cleveland, OH: The World Publishing Company.

Carle, E. (1984). *The very busy spider*. New York: Scholastic.

Choi, Y. (2001). *The name jar*. New York: Knopf.

Cisneros, S. (1984). *The house on Mango Street*. New York: Vintage Contemporaries.

del Castillo, R. G. (2002). *César Chávez: The struggle for justice/César Chávez: La lucha por la justicia*. Houston, TX: Piñata Books.

Dooley, N. (1991). *Everyone cooks rice*. New York: Carolrhoda Books, Inc.

Drew, D. (1988). *Somewhere in the universe*. Crystal Lake, IL: Rigby.

Fox, M. (1997). *Whoever you are*. San Diego, CA: Harcourt Brace.

García-Moliner, G. (1993). *En aguas profundas*. Boston: Houghton Mifflin.

Garza, C. L. (1996). *In my family/En mi familia*. San Francisco: Children's Book Press.

Gershator, D., & Gershator, P. (1995). *Bread is for eating*. New York: Scholastic.

Golden Opportunities. (2004). Barrington, IL: Rigby.

Goldstein, B. S. (Ed.). (1995). *What's on the menu?* New York: Puffin Books.

Gonzales-Bertrand, D. (1996). *Sip, slurp, soup, soup, caldo, caldo, caldo*. Houston, TX: Piñata Books.

González-Jensen, M. (1997a). *El maíz maravilloso de México*. Crystal Lake, IL: Rigby.

González-Jensen, M. (1997b). *Judge for a day*. Crystal Lake, IL: Rigby.

González-Jensen, M. (1997c). *Juez por un día*. Crystal Lake, IL: Rigby.

González-Jensen, M. (1997d). *Mexico's marvelous corn*. Crystal Lake, IL: Rigby.

Guthard, P. (1995). Ready for spaghetti. In B. Goldstein (Ed.), *What's on the menu?* (p. 13). New York: Puffin Books.

Hayes, J. (2005). *A spoon for every bite/Una cuchara para cada bocado*. El Paso, TX: Cinco Puntos Press.

Heller, R. (1985). *How to hide a butterfly and other insects*. New York: Grosset and Dunlap.

Hirsch, C. F. (2004). *To trade or not to trade*. Barrington, IL: Rigby.

In the deep. (2004). Barrington, IL: Rigby.

Jackson, I. (1998). *The big bug search*. New York: Scholastic.

Jenkins, R. (1998). *Growing a plant: A journal*. Crystal Lake, IL: Rigby.

Jiménez, F. (1997). *The circuit: Stories from the life of a migrant child*. Albuquerque, NM: University of New Mexico Press.

Jiménez, F. (1998). *La mariposa*. Boston: Houghton Mifflin.

Jiménez, F. (2001). *Breaking through*. Boston: Houghton Mifflin.

Kennedy, X. J. (1995). Italian noodles. In B. Goldstein (Ed.), *What's on the menu?* (p. 12). New York: Puffin Books.

Kite, P. (1997). *Insectos asombrosos*. Boston: Houghton Mifflin.

Kovacs, D. (1987). *A day under water*. New York: Scholastic.

Krauss, R. (1945). *The carrot seed*. New York: Scholastic.

Krauss, R. (1978). *La semilla de zanahoria*. New York: Scholastic.

Krull, K. (2003). *Harvesting hope: The story of César Chávez*. New York: Harcourt.

Leonhardt, A. (2000). *Ocean life: Tide pool creatures*. Austin, TX: Steck-Vaughn.

Los panes del mundo. (1993). New York: Scholastic.

Lucca, M. (2001). *Plants grow from seeds*. Washington, DC: National Geographic Society.

Lucca, M. (2003). *De las semillas nacen las plantas*. Washington, DC: National Geographic Society.

Maguire, A. (1999a). *Todos somos especiales*. León, Spain: Editorial Everest.

Maguire, A. (1999b). *We're all special*. León, Spain: Editorial Everest.

Marzollo, J. (1996). *I'm a seed*. Carmel, CA: Hampton-Brown.

McMillan, B. (1988). *Growing colors*. New York: William Morrow & Co.

McMillan, B. (1991). *Eating fractions*. New York: Scholastic.

Merriam, E. (1995). In the mood for a favorite food. In B. Goldstein (Ed.), *What's on the menu?* (p. 10). New York: Puffin Books.

Morris, A. (1989). *Bread, bread, bread*. New York: Mulberry Books.

Morrison, R. (1998). *How does it grow?* Crystal Lake, IL: Rigby.

Nikola-Lisa, W. (1997). *America: My land, your land, our land*. New York: Lee & Low Books.

Nye, N. (1997). *Sitti's secret*. New York: Aladdin Paperbacks.

Oppenheim, J. (1996). *Have you seen bugs?* New York: Scholastic.

Our book of maps. (2004). Barrington, IL: Rigby.

Palacios, A. (1997). *One city, one school, many foods*. Crystal Lake, IL: Rigby.

Pallotta, J. (1998). *The butterfly counting book*. New York: Scholastic.

Paulsen, G. (1995a). *La tortillería*. Orlando, FL: Harcourt, Brace & Company.

Paulsen, G. (1995b). *The tortilla factory*. New York: Harcourt, Brace & Company.

Pile, M. (2005). *Mexican immigration*. Washington, DC: National Geographic.

Prelutsky, J. (1996). Spaghetti! Spaghetti! In J. D. Cooper & J. J. Pikulski (Eds.), *Celebrate*. Boston: Houghton Mifflin.

Reid, M., & Chessen, B. (1998). *Bugs, bugs, bugs*. New York: Scholastic.

Rice, H. (2001). *Sea lights*. Katonah, NY: Richard C. Owen.

Rodríguez, L. (1997). *América is her name*. Willimantic, CT: Curbstone Press.

Salinas, B. (1998). *The three pigs/Los tres cerdos: Nacho, Tito, and Miguel*. Oakland, CA: Piñata Publications.

Sands, S. (1997). *Oceans*. New York: Kids Discover.

Sandved, K. B. (1996). *The butterfly alphabet*. New York: Scholastic.

Shulman, L. (2004). *Making pizza with math*. Barrington, IL: Rigby.

Smith, D. J. (2002). *If the world were a village*. Toronto: Kids Can Press.

Soto, G. (1995). *Chato's kitchen*. New York: Scholastic.

Soto, G. (1997). *Buried onions*. San Diego, CA: Harcourt, Brace & Company.

Torres, L. (1995a). *El sancocho del sábado*. New York: Farrar, Straus and Giroux.

Torres, L. (1995b). *Saturday sancocho*. New York: Farrar, Straus and Giroux.

Trapani, I. (1996). *The itsy bitsy spider*. Boston: Houghton Mifflin.

Tsang, N. (2003). *Rice all day*. Barrington, IL: Rigby.

Waber, B. (1972). *Ira sleeps over*. Boston: Houghton Mifflin.

Wachter, J. (2004). *In the ocean*. Barrington, IL: Rigby.

Wainman, M. (1982). *One elephant, two elephants*. Port Coquitlam, Canada: Class Size Books.

Walker, C. (1992a). *Plants and seeds*. Bothell, WA: The Wright Group.

Walker, C. (1992b). *Seeds grow*. Bothell, WA: The Wright Group.

Walker, C. (1995). *Plantas y semillas* (G. Andújar, Trans.). Bothell, WA: The Wright Group.

Weil, A. (2004). *Water all around the earth*. Barrington, IL: Rigby.

Whitney, N. (1996). *The tiny dot*. Boston: Houghton Mifflin.

Windsor, J. (1999a). *Big animals in the sea*. Crystal Lake, IL: Rigby.

Windsor, J. (1999b). *On the seashore*. Crystal Lake, IL: Rigby.

Index